HOW TO RAISE BUSINESS FINANCE

In this Series

How to Pass Exams Without Anxiety
How to Raise Business Finance
How to Get That Job
How to Use a Library
How to Live & Work in America
How to Live & Work in Australia
How to Enjoy Retirement
How to Claim State Benefits
How to Help Your Child at School
How to Get a Job Abroad
How to Survive at College
How to Prepare for Leaving School

other titles in preparation

How To Books General Editor Roland Seymour

How To...

Raise Business Finance

Peter Ibbetson

Northcote House

First published in 1987 by Northcote House Publishers Ltd,
Harper & Row House, Estover Road, Plymouth PL6 7PZ,
United Kingdom. Tel: Plymouth (0752) 705251. Telex: 45635.

British Library Cataloguing in Publication Data

Ibbetson, Peter
How to raise business finance. — (How to series)
1. Small business — Great Britain — Finance
I. Title
658.1'522 HG4027.7
ISBN 0-7463-0338-6

Printed and bound in Great Britain by
Biddles Ltd, Guildford and King's Lynn

Contents

Introduction	6
1 The Right Type of Finance for You	7
2 The Financier's Viewpoint	19
3 Presenting Your Case: Trading Finance	35
4 Presenting Your Case: Longer-Term Finance	49
5 Research and Development Finance	65
6 Factoring	76
7 Leasing	83
8 Finance for Exporters	91
9 Government Grants and Assistance	107
10 As You Go Along	119
11 When Things Go Right	127
12 When Things Go Wrong	131
13 Who to Contact	
Lending sources	139
Goverment sources	141
Other bodies	144
Glossary	147
Some Useful Reference Books	150
Index	151

Introduction

Where do you begin? You know you need finance — but what type — who do you approach — and how do you impress them into backing your business?

From the outset, let's get one thing straight. All financiers have one thing in common — they are all there to make a profit — mostly from lending money. They are as keen to lend as you are to borrow — providing your venture looks viable and they are happy you can repay your borrowing. That's in your interests too, though. It's no use going ahead with your business plans blindly unaware of the financial implications, nor proceeding in the knowledge that the figures don't really add up. At the end of the day there's only one loser.

It pays, then, to prepare and present your case fully, both to convince yourself that your efforts will be worthwhile, and to convince your backer that his investment in you will be safe.

This handbook is designed to help you through the planning and preparatory stages, show the various types of finance available, and how to put your package together to help your financier's assessment.

We first look briefly at the types of finance available, then consider the best way of presenting your case. Alternative sources of finance are reviewed and, once everything is up and running, the way forward is discussed. A directory of who to contact, and a glossary of references can be found at the end of the guide.

Remember — your financier is really on your side and not in competition with you. If you help him, he will be only too delighted to assist you.

1
The Right Type of Finance for You

Choosing the right type of finance is very much like selecting the right-sized bit for your electric drill. All will make a hole, but only the correct size will do the job properly. It's just the same with finance; all types of finance will provide you with the cash, but only the right type will have the right repayment terms, interest rates and so on for your needs.

To ensure you get the best deal, then, it's up to *you* to consider:

- What your real requirements are.
- Which financial package will suit you best.

This chapter will help steer you through the various 'groups' of finance available in the market. Having decided which is right for you, you can then refer to the appropriate chapter for more detailed guidance on putting your package together.

You should always keep in mind:

1. Purpose
2. Cost
3. Repayment
4. Balance sheet stability
5. Incentives

WHY IS THE RIGHT CHOICE IMPORTANT?

1. Purpose

Normally finance is split into some form of **loan**, or some form of trading **overdraft**. If you are purchasing a capital or non-trading item — for example, a machine — then a loan is appropriate. Unless capital and trading finance are kept separate it is difficult to monitor how trading is progressing.

It is sensible to look at the funding of such a capital item over its productive life. Again, let's consider a machine. If its working life will be five years — during which time it will be contributing to profits — why not arrange a loan with repayments spread over five years? After all that's really how you 'purchase' your staff. You may wish to retain flexibility. Suppose you need a specialist machine which will be quickly outdated and which you may want to replace in the short term. In this case a rental or 'leasing' arrangement may be appropriate.

2. Cost

Cost will vary widely from one type of facility to another. As a starting point, unauthorised borrowing (for example taken on overdraft without the lender's agreement) will prove far more expensive than an authorised facility. So, sort it out *before* you draw it.

Overdrafts are charged at a percentage over **base rate**, and will vary as base rate moves up and down.

Loans on the other hand can be either: **variable**, i.e. a percentage over base rate, or **structured**, i.e. charged at an agreed flat rate from the outset.

Special schemes will normally be a little more expensive, but will have added frills which can make the extra cost worthwhile.

Your main consideration here will be the choice between a variable or structured loan. From a cost point of view the major factor is the level of interest rates when you take out the loan. If they are particularly low, it is worth choosing a structured facility, and tying in these low rates for the term of the loan. But if rates are high, it pays to stay with a variable facility; the cost will reduce as interest rates fall in the market. The structured loan does have the advantage that you know what it will cost from the outset; with the variable loan the cost may go up or down.

Fig. 1.1 How interest rates can move

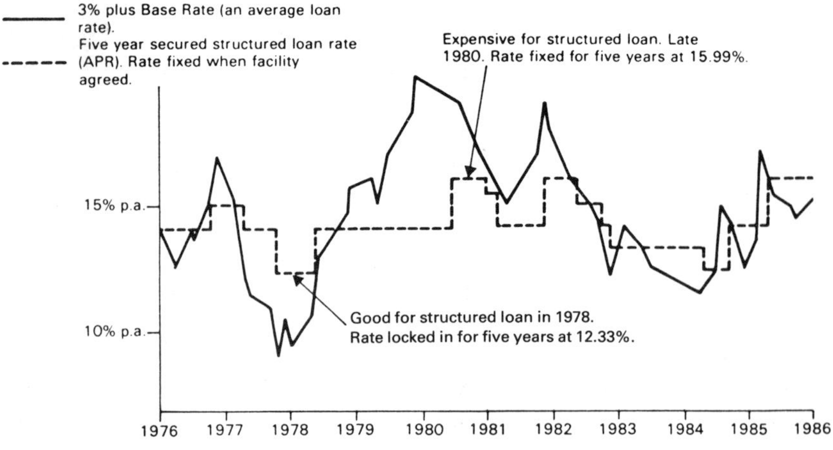

Figure 1.1 shows how interest rates moved between 1976 and 1986, and at which times it would have paid to take a structured loan.

The problem is to predict what will happen to interest rates in the future? Any good financial newspaper or magazine will give you some idea.

A trading requirement, which will swing between **debit** and **credit**, is well suited to an overdraft. You pay interest only when you are in debit. There is little sense in borrowing on one account whilst another is in credit; in effect you are paying to borrow your own money. But it is important to separate capital funding and trading monies; you may find yourself with a trading account often, even always, in credit, whilst paying interest say on your five year loan. You have two options:

1. Decide how much surplus cash you can allot to the capital item, and reduce the loan, or
2. Come to an arrangement with your lender whereby you pay only a nominal amount of interest (say 1% or 2%) on whatever element of borrowing is covered by credit balances elsewhere. For example:

Borrowing	**Credit balances**
(Loan a/c—5 years) £50,000	(Current a/c) never falling below, say, £20,000

You pay normal interest on £30,000 and nominal interest (say 2%) on £20,000. This arrangement is known as **set off**. When the figures are large enough it is widely used, but your lender is hardly likely to suggest it! It's up to you to make the move.

An agreed loan facility is often slightly cheaper than an overdraft—but remember, unless you are able to negotiate a set off arrangement, you will get no allowance for any credit balances.

Shop around. Different lenders will charge different rates for very similar services. Usually the banks rank amongst the cheapest, but even these vary from one to another.

The cheapest form of finance is to use other people's money, i.e. creditors, but you need to weigh up the value of discounts for early payment. Similarly, poor control of debtors — those who owe *you* money — may well mean you have to borrow elsewhere at some cost to fund your trading, so it pays to keep on top of the paperwork. If this proves time-consuming or difficult **factoring** may be worth considering.

3. Repayment

None of us particularly enjoy owing money, but we wouldn't think of repaying our mortgage from our first two years' salary — simply because it would leave us unacceptably short elsewhere! So it is with business finance. You must consider, and decide upon, a realistic repayment schedule and choose your finance accordingly.

This complements the view that a capital item or fixed asset should be 'bought' over its working life. There is no sense in borrowing, say over two years, thereby stretching cash flow to the point where your trading ability is restricted. It may mean lost contracts, pressing creditors, returned cheques and similar nightmares, when you *could* borrow over five years and experience no such problems. As a guide to what borrowing will cost you the following table shows — in pounds — the monthly sum including interest needed to repay a loan of £1,000 with interest debited quarterly:

Number of Years for Repayment	INTEREST RATES					
	10%	11%	12%	13%	14%	15%
1	£87.87	£88.33	£88.79	£89.25	£89.70	£90.16
2	£46.10	£46.56	£47.01	£47.47	£47.93	£48.40
3	£32.23	£32.70	£33.16	£33.62	£34.09	£34.57
4	£25.32	£25.79	£26.28	£26.76	£27.42	£27.73
5	£21.20	£21.69	£22.18	£22.68	£23.18	£23.69
6	£18.45	£18.98	£19.49	£20.00	£20.51	£21.04
7	£16.56	£17.06	£17.59	£18.11	£18.65	£19.19
8	£15.10	£15.65	£16.19	£16.73	£17.28	£17.84
9	£14.03	£14.57	£15.12	£15.67	£16.24	£16.81
10	£13.17	£13.72	£14.28	£14.85	£15.43	£16.02

For example a borrowing of £10,000 at 12% over two years would cost £470.10 per month. Over five years the monthly repayments would be £221.80, assuming that base rate remained unchanged for a variable facility or, that you had opted for a structured facility. If you do opt for a structured loan, the rate will be quoted as, say, '7½% flat — APR 14.17%'. The rate you should compare and work your figures out on is the APR (Annual Percentage Rate). With a structured loan, in repayment terms, at least you know exactly what the monthly repayments will be, irrespective of interest movements in the money markets.

Capital Repayment Holidays may be available and appropriate if you are starting a business. Under a Holiday arrangement, you only have to cover interest for the initial period of the loan (up to two years in some cases). This can help if you expect cash flow to be tight to start with, but expect to make reasonable profits later on.

4. Balance Sheet Stability

This is probably the last thing you're thinking about just now, but it's still important. Chapter 2 looks at the way your prospective financier will view your Balance Sheet. Often the type and term of finance you take will have a material effect on how these appear:

- Solvency
- Liquidity

This might seem a bit theoretical, but often the Balance Sheet and Profit and Loss Statements are the *only* track record your financier will have. He will certainly place a lot of reliance on them, so you must consider how they will look.

The common plea, 'But my Balance Sheet is always drawn up for the taxman — that's why I always show a loss,' is no comfort to a prospective lender. After all, your repayment is supposed to be coming out of profits.

5. Incentives

Particularly when you are starting up, any help you can get is worth considering. The Government is the main incentive provider. It gives grants and support for a variety of purposes, to encourage specific types of industry, draw business to certain areas, create employment, and so on. A synopsis of what's available can be found in Chapter 9. Don't simply rely on the financier to point these out — he may not even be aware of some of them.

"We're here on a capital repayment holiday."

CASH INJECTIONS

Cash injections come from:

- Family sources
- Outside sources

Family funds will be considered either as money introduced permanently into a business venture, or as a loan — often a 'director's loan'. Outside funds will usually be in the form of loans or equity, although Government grants may provide a simple permanent cash injection.

Cash injections are certainly very important. In the early stages they will be the sole components forming your **capital base**. As time passes and profits are made, this base should be increased by retained profits. But at the outset, the cash injections will be seen as the level of the investors' **commitment**. Obviously, the greater the proprietor's commitment, the more comfortable a lender will feel, and directors' loans, for example, should be considered as **quasi capital** i.e. semi-permanent monies, rather than a short-term loan which is going to be withdrawn at the earliest possible opportunity. That would hardly demonstrate commitment and confidence in the future! Quite often, a lender will seek a **postponement** over family loan monies, to prevent them being repaid before the lender is repaid.

Apart from commitment value, cash injections are important, as they will provide cost-free or cheap finance, whether for fixed asset purchases or for trading. Clearly, the lower finance costs can be kept, the higher your profits will be.

CREDITORS/DEBTORS AND DISCOUNTS

Using other people's money is a very cost-effective method of funding trading. In simple terms, the longer credit you take, matched by efficient collection of your own debtors, the lower your borrowing requirement. Thus, the lower your finance costs will be.

The more highly regarded high street stores are notoriously skilful at managing their creditors and debtors. Generally they will take payment in cash, yet in many cases take several months' credit from their own suppliers. In other words they are using *your* money to fund *their* trading.

You must get this balance right, though. You don't want to alienate your creditors by delaying payment too long. Nor do you want to upset your debtors (customers) by demanding they pay up at once. Both would start looking elsewhere for business. Research the market and see what the accepted norms are, first. Then set your own targets. As a guide, the following examples are roughly what you should be aiming for:

Small scale Construction Work	50-60 days*
Food and Drink Distributors	5-15 days
Electrical Industry	65-75 days
Metals industry	75-85 days
Transport Distributors	15-25 days
Printing Industry	60-70 days
Textile & Footwear Manufacture	35-45 days
Retail Industry	
Carpet Distributors	39 days
D.I.Y.	12 days
High Street Trading	14 days
Chemists	42 days
Jewellers	15 days
Sports Goods	35 days
Toy Distributors	50 days
Services	
Advertising	51 days
Computing	65 days
Cleaning (Contract)	57 days

* Periods represent the average number of days taken before accounts are paid.

Liquidity

The liquidity angle is relevant, too. You should always be able to see how you are going to settle your creditors if need be, whether from stock sales, debtors, or even from bank borrowing.

If you simply *cannot* pay creditors who start pressing, continuance of the business may be threatened. Chapter 12 looks at such eventualities.

To encourage you to pay early, your creditors may offer a 2½% to 5% discount for prompt payment; you may wish to consider a similar incentive for your own debtors. Do work out the financial implications, though. For example, a 5% discount for settlement now of a debt otherwise due for payment in three months time is equivalent to 20% interest per annum. In times of high interest rates, it would pay you to *offer* such a discount. Similarly, in times of low interest rates, it would be worthwhile *accepting* such a facility.

A final consideration should be your competitors terms of credit. You must be willing to match or better these if you want to remain competitive in the market.

PROFIT ISN'T CASH

'If you've made a profit of £20,000, why has your borrowing increased?' This questions is often asked by confused bank managers, and it baffles many customers. The simple answer is that more cash was spent than was generated from profits. Perhaps a fixed asset was purchased, higher levels of stock were being carried, or the amount due from debtors had increased.

The 'worth' of the business may have increased (greater asset value), but the bank position may have deteriorated.

There is nothing at all wrong with this, as long as:

- The position is understood, and
- A source of repayment of the borrowing can be seen.

It is important to understand that 'profit' does not necessarily mean an improved cash position. It *may* do, but much depends upon your trading pattern and the need to replace fixed assets.

TRADING FINANCE

In deciding the most appropriate type of finance you first need to analyse your precise needs.

Trading finance will be required for instance, when you need to borrow to cover the cost of buying stock for future sales; those sales will in due course be your means of repayment.

Unfortunately life is never quite that simple. In the real world, the position is complicated by creditors, debtors, uncertain sales patterns, and other factors.

The result is that:

- You are never quite sure exactly how much you will need or when.
- There may be times when you need no facilities at all, and it is pointless paying for unnecessary finance at such times.

You therefore need flexibility. You need a facility which is there when you need it, but for which you are not charged when you don't. An overdraft is the usual vehicle to meet these needs.

Chapter 3 looks more at how the overdraft should work, and how you should present your case.

LONGER TERM FINANCE

If you want to fund one particular item — for instance a machine — you know exactly how much you need, when, and how repayment can be handled. For this, a loan is clearly more appropriate. It can be moulded to your needs, over a term which recognises the expected life of the asset. It may, for example, include a capital repayment holiday arrangement, mentioned earlier in this Chapter.

Under 'cost' we have already introduced the concept of:

- Structured Loans
- Variable Rate Loans

A decison will have to be made as to which is more appropriate.

Chapter 4 considers the approach for Longer Term Finance.

There is nothing mystical about splitting your financing arrangements into fluctuating (i.e. overdraft) and fixed term. It is no different from what you would do in a personal situation. You would use an overdraft to cover day-to-day bills pending your salary cheque, and a loan to cover your car purchase, over say three years. The corporate situation is exactly the same.

DEVELOPMENT FINANCE

The problems associated with Research and Development often require a greater degree of understanding than in more day-to-day matters. In addition to market research costs, research and prototype costs may have to be borne long before any cash income is generated.

By the production stage, the proprietors' own funds have often been exhausted and financiers are frequently asked for 100% support.

This may involve simple overdraft facilities but often a capital injection is warranted and this may involve giving up some of your **equity** (shares).

The planning process is particularly important with Research and Development. Chapter 5 considers this in more depth along with the various stages and types of finance available.

FACTORING

Factoring is really a collection of three distinct services:

- Sales accounting
- Debtor collection and bad debt protection
- Advances against invoices

The 'advances against invoices' aspect is a recognised source of trading finance in appropriate instances. A typical prospective case may be suffering from:

— existing poor collection of debtors
—unacceptable levels of bad debts
— strained cash flow
— stretched management time due to excess time involved in sales accounting.

The mechanics involve the factoring company buying the customer's book debts on an on-going basis. This provides cash straight away rather than having to wait for the debts to fall due under the agreed terms of trade.

Factoring is not the answer in all cases, but it can be a useful method of raising working capital.

Invoice Discounting offers similar opportunities and is considered, together with factoring, in more depth in Chapter 6.

LEASING

Leasing is a form of medium-term finance for fixed-asset funding. The leasing company buys the asset and then 'leases' it back at an agreed rental. There are two main types of leasing —

- Finance leases
- Operating leases

Both are discussed in more detail in Chapter 7. In general, they are aimed to satisfy similar needs and offer similar benefits.

Since leasing takes advantage of 'tax manipulation' it is complex and relies on specific balance sheet year ends. But it is worth exploring if the company:

- Does not pay Corporation Tax (because it is either not profitable or tax exempt).
- Does not wish to commit any resources for a deposit.
- Requires a fixed asset, often subject to regular technological updating, such as hi-tech equipment, but car leasing is also very popular.

The leasing company can often construct a package which makes leasing more attractive than outright purchase — whether for cash, or on loan. The simple fact that ownership does not, in the initial period, pass to your company, should not dissuade you from seeking a quote.

WHO TO APPROACH

Your first line of approach should be your existing, or prospective, bank manager. He is unlikely to charge you for his advice, and in fact will probably be quite pleased to have the chance to assess your needs and provide facilities. In any event, he can direct you to the most appropriate type of finance, and will often know the financier personally.

Most of the major banks have subsidiaries which are specialists in leasing, factoring and so on. Your bank manager will be happy to introduce you to them without the conflict of perhaps losing your business.

An accountant would charge for his advice, but a modest fee could be money well spent. In the longer term, if your business does succeed, you will need an accountant anyway so an early introduction may well be worthwhile. Your bank manager will probably be able to put you in touch with a good accountant, if you wish.

CHECKLIST	
Consider	Purpose Term Cost Ability to repay
Choose	The most appropriate finance in your opinion, and have good reasons for your choice
Research	Any available grants and incentives
Seek	Advice from a professional — in the first instance the Bank Manager

2
The Financier's Viewpoint

Before any approach for finance is made it is *vital* that you appreciate the lender's perspective. An understanding of how the financier's mind is ticking will ensure:

- That the borrowers are fully prepared
- That calls for further information are minimised
- That a prompt decision is forthcoming
- That the best arrangement can be negotiated in terms both of cost and commitment of security

FIRST IMPRESSIONS

The lender will want to consider your past performance (your 'track record') and future prospects, but will be influenced immediately, rightly or wrongly, by the first impressions that you give him.

The late arrival for interview will sow doubts of organisational ability — will the borrowing be repaid on time? Similarly, an untidy appearance or inadequately thought-out proposition will undermine confidence.

Proper preparation and a little time spent anticipating the first meeting with the lender will pay you worthwhile dividends.

TRACK RECORD

Whether you are a personal or business customer, existing account holder, or new client, the lender will consider your track record — or past history, previous successes/failures — before deciding about the future.

For business customers, past performance is clearly evidenced in the balance sheets and profit and loss accounts. The lender's assessment of these may be quite different from yours — especially where he does not fully understand your particular industry. Be ready to take the initiative in emphasising and explaining the accounts; don't just let the lender make his own, often wrong, judgment.

As a guide, the lender would normally be looking at the following:

- Commitment (or gearing)
- Liquidity
- Profitability

Commitment (or gearing)

This is the ratio between borrowed funds and shareholders' or partnership funds. In simple terms it is the share capital (plus accumulated profit and loss balance) compared to the amount borrowed from outside lenders — banks, HP companies, under leasing contracts, mortgage companies, and so on. As a rule of thumb, lenders are not keen to see their own involvement exceed that of the shareholders, i.e. a gearing exceeding 1:1.

Frequently, however, there are several adjustments which can quite legitimately be made to improve the position, and which you should be ready to justify. These involve in particular:

- Directors' loans
- Hidden reserves

Often there will be directors' loans in the business. If you see these as a long-term investment then you should emphasise and be prepared to accept their permanence in the business. This enables them to be treated as quasi capital rather than borrowed monies.

Similarly, the capital base can be improved by introducing any **hidden reserves** into the balance sheet. These may include undervaluations which have been left for some time, usually for tax reasons, at a figure very much below the true current market price.

There is no need to enter the proper figure in the balance sheet, but it pays to point it out to the lender since it will effectively increase your profit and loss balance, and hence the shareholders' funds, with a resultant improvement in gearing. Against this, the lender will often regard assets such as goodwill, patents and short leases as **intangible**. As such he will discount them from the balance sheet, effectively reducing your capital base and worsening the gearing.

Fig. 2.1 represents the sort of gearing adjustment you should be considering.

Liquidity

Capital repayment of any facility, whether overdraft or loan, flows from cashflow — hence the lender's concern with this. This aspect receives further consideration under Repayment later in this section, but in general terms an accurate and realistic awareness of the liquid position will help inspire confidence.

Fig. 2.1 — Gearing Adjustment Example

BALANCE SHEET

Assets	Freehold Premises (current value £40,000)	£25,000	
	Fixtures and Fittings	£10,000	
	Goodwill	£ 7,000	
	Current Assets (Stock, Debtors, etc)	£18,000	
			£60,000
Liabilities	Bank Overdraft	£19,000	
	Creditors	£14,000	
	Hire Purchase	£ 4,000	
	Directors' Loans	£ 6,000	
			£43,000
			£17,000
Represented by	Share Capital	£ 5,000	
	Profit & Loss	£12,000	
			£17,000
Gearing			
Pre-adjustment	Shareholders' Funds	£17,000	
	Borrowed Monies	£29,000	
	Gearing 29:17 (*more* than 1:1, and not very satisfactory).		
Post-adjustment	Shareholders' Funds	£17,000	
	Plus Hidden Reserve	£15,000	
	Plus Directors' Loans	£ 6,000	£38,000
	Less Goodwill		£ 7,000
			£31,000
	Borrowed Monies (Bank & HP)		£23,000
	Gearing now 23:31 (*less* than 1:1, and far more satisfactory).		

Profitability
One of the major sources of cash into the business will, hopefully, be from profits. The lender will therefore concentrate upon:

- The steady maintenance of **gross profit margins**, which should be in line with the particular industry as a whole. Be ready to explain any variances from the norm.

- The control of **overhead expenditure** — regarded as a sign of how well the management are in control. A useful comparison in this respect is that of the **Net** profit margin against the **Gross** profit margin. Tighter overhead control will be shown by the percentage net profit figure growing more (or slipping less) than the gross profit margin. Again, a ready explanation should be to hand for any departures from the ideal (see in Fig. 2.2).

Fig. 2.2 Overheads expenditure control

$$\text{Gross Profit Margin} = \frac{GP}{Sales} \times 100$$

$$\text{Net Profit Margin} = \frac{NP}{Sales} \times 100$$

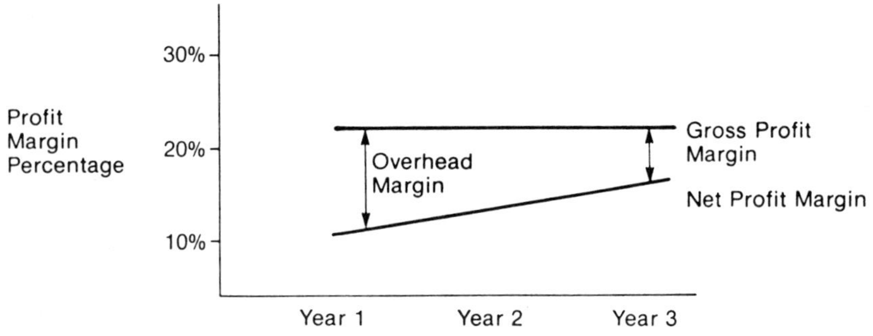

Comment: Both GP and NP Margins improving, but NP Margin growing at a greater rate than GP Margin — indicating tighter overhead control.

PURPOSE — THE RIGHT TYPE OF FINANCE

It is in your own interest to seek the type of finance most suited to your needs, although clearly it is wise to seek the lender's advice. The lender should therefore be appraised fully of the purpose behind the borrower's approach; withholding relevant information will help no-one.

The financial need will normally fall into three categories:

- **Short term** — such as an overdraft or bridging loan.
- **Medium term** — such as a three-year loan for capital purchases.
- **Long term** — such as mortgage finance.

Aside from obvious considerations such as legality, the lender will also wish to ensure that both the *term* and *type* of finance match the purpose. It would be inappropriate for instance to fund a day-to-day trading requirement by a five year loan. Conversely, it would not be appropriate to fund a capital item, with an estimated life of seven years, on overdraft.

Often, however, a borrower's needs will be *split* between capital *and* trading requirements — especially in start up situations. As discussed in the previous Chapter, it is sensible to fund capital items over their useful life, whereas a trading requirement must be seen as a day-to-day facility, swinging between debit and credit.

Providing your differing requirements are identified and kept separate, you will be able to monitor your trading position closely. The inappropriate funding of capital items on overdraft will merely cloud the issue, and in new businesses much-needed working capital will be locked up in capital investments.

It is important then for you to give some thought to matching finance to need *before* approaching the lender. The lender will then have a soundly based proposal to consider which recognises all the relevant points as you see them.

PROJECT VIABILITY

Any financier is guaranteed to introduce a sobering influence into any project! Quite naturally, he won't share the same blind optimism as the borrower, and will need to be convinced of the viability of the proposition towards which he is asked to lend.

A **Business Plan** may well already have been compiled but, in particular, the lender will wish to see:

1. evidence of level of borrowing
2. profit forecast
3. break-even calculation
4. the forecast on which the proposed level of borrowing is based. In the case of a capital purchase, this is a relatively simple exercise, *viz* —

Cost	£
Less money already available	£
	£

To justify a trading finance requirement (overdraft) may not be so simple, as there will inevitably be uncertainties, but the borrower should still prepare some form of Cash Flow Forecast.

Fig. 2.3

Cashflow Forecast For

Branch	name of company, firm etc

Enter month						
	Projected	**Actual**	Projected	**Actual**	Projected	**Actual**
Receipts						
Sales – Cash						
Sales – Debtors						
Loans						
Other receipts						
A Total receipts						
Payments						
Cash purchases						
To creditors						
Wages and salaries (net)						
PAYE/NIC						
Capital items						
Rent/rates						
Services						
HP/leasing repayments						
Bank/finance charges						
Loan repayments						
VAT (net)						
Corporation tax, etc						
Dividend						
B Total payments						
Opening bank balance						
Add to B if overdrawn Subtract from B if credit						
C Total						
D Closing bank balance (Difference between A&C)						

For the period

From To

						Total	
Projected	**Actual**	Projected	**Actual**	Projected	**Actual**	Projected	**Actual**

1. Cash Flow Forecast

Ideally this should be drawn up on a monthly basis. It should indicate the anticipated sources of income for the month, together with the anticipated expenditures, and conclude with the anticipated shortfall—i.e. the borrowing requirement. Most lenders have blank Cash Flow Forecast forms available for completion. The example in fig. 2.3 is pretty standard.

The practical uses of a cash flow are discussed in Chapter 3, but the following ground rules are important:

(a) **Be pessimistic rather than optimistic.** It is far better to over-estimate a requirement than to under-estimate it. An **over-estimate** will see the borrowing operating well within the agreed facility and this will be translanted as demonstrating keen management control. On the other hand an **under-estimate** will result in pressure on the facility, with the likelihood of frequent 'excesses', and the possibility of dishonoured cheques — all of which will rightly create an impression of poor financial control. The temptation to minimise a borrowing request—in the mistaken belief that financiers wish to minimise their lending— should be resisted.

(b) **A month by month Cash Flow Forecast does not take into account monthly timing differences.** It assumes payments out are made on the same day as payments in are received. In practice this is rarely the case— normally payments in and out will be relatively spread across the month. But some large payments (such as wages) may be made at the beginning of the month, in anticipation of funds flowing in later. In this case the 'net monthly requirement', whilst being accurate at the month end, will be understated for the middle of the month. The borrowing requirement request must reflect this if the eventualities mentioned in (a) are to be avoided.

The lender will not be aware of these finer details, and it is *your* job to anticipate any hiccups.

2. Profit Forecast

This will have been drawn up, probably several times, by the prospective borrower. Each time he will try to evidence an improved performance! The lender however will be looking for a *realistic* forecast which:

- uses margins largely in line with the industry norm.
- can justify the projected level of sales (market research).
- splits expenditure into *variable* costs (such as purchases and wages, to a degree, which, if sales levels are not achieved, can be reduced, and *fixed* costs (such as rates, electricity, heating) which will need to be paid regardless. (The split into variable and fixed costs will help you compile the Break Even Calculation — see (3) below).

The following **Projected Profit Forecast** format is the sort of approach the lender will be looking for:

Projected Profit Forecast for the period: January-December

Note 1	Projected Sales		£100,000
	Less Variable Costs of Sales:		
	Purchases	£20,000	
	Labour	£35,000	
	Total		£ 55,000
Note 2	Trading (or Gross) Profit		£ 45,000
	Less Fixed Overhead costs:		
	Rent and Rates	£10,000	
	Heating	£ 2,000	
	Lighting	£ 1,000	
	Telephone/Postage	£ 3,000	
	Insurance	£ 1,000	
	Professional Fees		
	Solicitor, Accountant, etc.	£ 2,000	
	Bank Interest	£ 4,000	
	Other likely expenses	£ 2,000	
	TOTAL		£ 25,000
Note 3	Net Profit — available to Directors' withdrawals/investment in Company etc.		£ 20,000

Again, the practical use of the profit projection will be considered in Chapter 3, but the lender will be particularly interested in the following points:

Note 1
Basis of projected sales. This should *not* be a pipe-dream. You must be able to offer the lender some clear evidence that your estimates are achievable.

Note 2
Gross Profit. By multiplying the anticipated Gross Profit figure x 100 and dividing by the projected sales figures you will get the Gross Profit margin:

$$\frac{\text{Gross Profit x 100}}{\text{Sales}} = \text{Gross Profit Margin (\%)}$$

This should be broadly in line with your industry norm. If not, the lender will want to know why — are sales being over/under costed, and so on.

Note 3

Net Profit. If all goes according to plan this is what your business is all about. You must remember that Corporation Tax may become payable on this profit, but essentially you must decide how much to take out by way of directors' withdrawals, and how much to leave invested in the business. Work out your realistic living expenses (i.e. your minimum likely withdrawals) and be ready to justify these to the lender. He will fully appreciate your wish, and indeed need, to 'earn a crust', but will equally advise retaining some profits in the business to ensure continuing growth, and less reliance in future on borrowed monies.

3. Break Even Calculation

Everything so far assumes that all will go according to plan. In your own interests, and certainly to satisfy the lender's worst fears, a 'break even calculation' should be drawn up. This shows how far the projections can slip before business ceases to be viable. The idea of a break-even is to see what minimum level of business you need to cover fixed costs.

An example best illustrates how it works. Let's assume sales are projected at £110,000 with a gross profit of £24,000. The gross profit margin is therefore 21.82%. Let's further assume that fixed overheads (including interest on borrowings) are estimated at £14,000. If the profit margin of 21.82% can be achieved then the minimum sales necessary to 'break even' will be as follows.

$$\frac{\text{Overheads x 100}}{\text{Gross Profit Margin}} = \frac{14000 \text{ x } 100}{21.82} = £64{,}162$$

If, on the other hand, the profit margin has to be reduced (i.e. goods sold cheaper) to keep sales up at £110,000, then the 'break even' margin will be:

$$\frac{\text{Overheads x 100}}{\text{Sales}} = \frac{1400000}{110000} = 12.73\%$$

It must be remembered, though, that a simple break-even will not leave anything over for directors' withdrawals, further investment, or any chance to reduce borrowing.

REPAYMENT

Repayment is what the lender will really be interested in. A confident assurance from yourself that everything will be 'all right on the night' will probably not satisfy him. The lender will need to be absolutely convinced that you can afford your proposals.

As a starting point, you must understand the difference between

- interest payments
- capital repayments

Running Costs

Under 'viability' we have already considered whether your projected profit will be enough to cover interest costs. This is a **revenue item** — much the same as electricity costs. Bank Interest is the charge for having and using borrowed monies. Just as you would deduct heating and lighting from your Profit and Loss Statement, so must you deduct Bank Interest.

By drawing up a Projected Profit Forecast you will already have looked at the question of Interest Cover. You must be able to show the lender that you can at least afford the cost of borrowing from him!

Don't forget to allow for a contingency margin if you are looking for a 'variable rate loan', in case interest rates should rise.

Ability to Repay

Actually repaying the money you have borrowed is a very different matter from 'affording the running costs.' The ability to deal with this **capital repayment** will depend upon how much *surplus* cash you can generate. In other words, how much will you be left with from profits, (and any other sources of cash) after any fixed asset purchases, funding of increased trading, and so on?

The interest payment will feature in your Profit and Loss Account, but capital repayments are Balance Sheet items. They are not a cost as such, and should not be looked at as 'money gone'.

It is much more positive to treat them as an investment. Let's say your company has a loan of £10,000 against an asset of £10,000. In the first year you generate £5,000 in Net Profit and decide to reduce the borrowing by the full £5,000. The Balance Sheet extract will now appear:

Liabilities	*Assets*
Loan £5,000	Asset £10,000

The balancing £5,000 will be referred to as **Shareholders' Funds**, or **Reserves**. Whilst you no longer have the £5,000 in cash, you as a shareholder now own more of the asset base.

This may seem rather academic, but it may serve as some comfort and put you in a more positive frame of mind when considering repayment with your lender.

In looking at your proposition the lender will look mainly for a practical approach. You must show that you can generate enough profit or cash to effect capital repayments and clear the borrowing over a realistic term.

To do this you must anticipate your cashflow position and draw up a **Projected Source and Application of Funds**. The following is the sort of format the lender will be looking for:

Source of Funds	
Projected net profit (before depreciation)	£
Anticipated Sales of Fixed Assets	£
Cash Injections — as Capital	£
as Loans	£
	A
Application of Funds	
Anticipated Fixed Asset Purchases	£
Proposed New Loan Repayments	£
Any extraordinary expenditure	£
	B

Working Capital Adjustment
to reflect any expected changes in trading patterns.

Stock — Increase (or Decrease)	£
Debtors — Increase (or Decrease)	£
Creditors — Increase (or Decrease)	£
	C

A less B, adjusted for C, will give the anticipated cash movement and show whether the loan capital repayments can be met.

Remember that the Projected Net Profit figure will already have accounted for all Revenue items, including interest costs. The practical application of this is considered in Chapter 3.

The lender will want you to have done your homework, and if you can convince him (as well as yourself) of your ability to repay, then half the battle is won.

SECURITY

Any self-respecting lender is going to want some kind of security — so don't be put off by such requests.

The lender will take the view that if your project is successful *you* will be the one to benefit most. On the other hand, if things go wrong he will want to ensure that he doesn't lose out. In other words, the whole thing is *your* gamble and the lender is merely there to help you out. He will

- be looking for some tangible security with a higher value than the lending
- consider the worst scenario and value the security with a pessimistic eye
- want something which is easy to value, which will maintain its value, and can be easily controlled.

Understand the lender's perspective here. Security is only of use to him if things go wrong, so that it would be pure folly on his part to over-value it.

Anticipate the items which will usually be asked for as collateral:

1. Land or Property
2. Stock and Debtors
3. Guarantees (supported or unsupported)

1. Land or Property

Generally recognised as the most stable type of security, it usually keeps its value well. Title can be legally vested in the lender's name, and he can exercise control. But there can be complications when a third party is involved. For instance, a **legal charge** over a matrimonial home must have the acknowledgment of the spouse although often one spouse will have no involvement whatsoever with the other spouse's business project. It is important then always to seek legal advice before pledging property. There will be costs associated both with the advice and the legal side of the security form, although experience frequently shows this to be money well spent.

Freehold property is usually sought by lenders as security. Short **leases** may well be assets in your own eyes, but the lender is likely to discount anything under, say, ten years unless situated in a prime location. Again, it is important to appreciate the lender's view, or be ready with a counter argument.

2. Stock and Debtors

Quite acceptable whether formally charged, or informally accepted as security. The problems here are those of value and control.

On the value side, the lender will have to take a pessimistic view. He may well consider stock and debtors to be worth under half the market value you believe is fair. Remember, though, that if the lender has to realise the value of stock and debtors himself because your business has failed, this will be an expensive exercise, and stock may be auctioned at well below market values. The problems will be worse still if the stock is specialised, out of date or damaged.

With debtors — especially if they are not 'spread' across a lot of small names — there may be a sizeable element of bad debts. Indeed, this may be why your business efforts have floundered in the first place.

Appreciate the lender's situation — if things do go wrong he naturally wants to ensure he is fully covered; only by building in a margin can he do so. Be realistic in your own assessment, and work with the lender, not against him.

3. Guarantees

You will often be asked to provide a guarantee either in addition to, or in the absence of, any other security. Frequently a guarantee will be taken to tie in your commitment, which is precisely what it does. In signing a standard guarantee form you surrender virtually all your rights, and banks do call up guarantees from time to time. They are seen as the easiest form of security to take, but the hardest to realise.

Ensure that, at the very least, you read and understand the small print. If possible seek legal advice.

INTEREST AND FEE

We have already accepted that lenders are in the market to make a profit. Be ready then to pay:

- An arrangement or commitment fee
- A fair rate of interest

The arrangement fee will normally be around ½% to 1% of the amount borrowed. The interest rate will typically be 3% to 4% over the lender's Base Rate, depending upon the risk and amount of security you can provide.

Don't necessarily just accept the figures sought by the lender — be ready to negotiate. He will always start at the top and often be prepared to come down a little.

Indeed, if you fail to haggle you may well leave the impression of poor business acumen. A wish for sensible negotiation, on the other hand, will be respected.

If it makes the pill any easier to swallow, most lenders will be prepared to add the fee to the loan, thus spreading the payment over the term of the loan. Be ready to suggest this, if it will suit you better.

WOULD YOU LEND?

'Would *you* lend?' — this is the acid test. If it was your money, would you lend it? If not, why not?

Are there any aspects which are not clear? If so, clarify them.

Are there any questions that you would ask? If so, have answers ready. Your prospective lender is bound to ask for them.

Put yourself in the lender's chair:

'How much have you got?''

Would YOU Lend the Money?	
First impressions	Do YOU look right? Does your proposition look right?
Track Record	Details of your background ready? Details of your Company's background ready?
Purpose	Right type of finance? Thought about it properly?
Project viability	Ready to prove it? Projected Profit Forecast? Projected Cash Flow? Break-Even?
Repayment	Are you convinced it's possible?
Security	Thought about it? What security is available? What's it really worth?
Interest and fee	Ready to negotiate?
Would YOU lend?	No final questions? No last nagging doubts?

3 Presenting Your Case: Trading Finance

This Chapter is aimed at helping you to put together your package for trading finance, working through a fairly typical example from start to finish.

Whilst it is obviously unlikely that your own proposition will fall precisely into the model, it does cover most eventualities, but you must consider it flexibly and be ready to make any adjustments as befit your case.

EXAMPLE: CHOICE OF FINANCE

To set the scene let's assume you have the opportunity to buy a greeting card manufacturer's business.

The business was started two years ago. Fig. 3.1 shows the latest Balance Sheet and Profit and Loss Statements. You feel that the business, as it stands, is tired, but you have contacts in the field and optimistic ideas of what can be achieved, even though an increase in turnover will mean more staff, and extra business will only be won by cutting margins.

Let's assume you have sufficient cash to buy the business. All you need is enough funding to support your day-to-day trading.

The immediate indications point towards the need for an overdraft. Money will be coming in and going out. It may be that at some stages you will be in credit, whilst at other times you will need something to fall back on.

You need a facility to cater for this — an overdraft.

PRICING — PIPE DREAM OR REALITY

Firstly, look at the way the business has fared over the past two years. If you are starting out afresh, look at the performances of similar firms in the recent past. How is the industry as a whole doing?

Research into greeting card manufacturing might show:

Average Gross Profit	30.0%
Average Net Profit	6.1%
Average Liquidity	1.6%
Stock Turnover	54 days
Debtor Period	65 days

This business at present shows:

Gross Profit Margin	34.6%
Net Profit Margin	3.8%
Liquidity	1.04%
Stock Turnover	52 days
Debtor Period	54 days

These figures suggest that, whilst gross margins are acceptable, control of overheads is poor. In the circumstances, directors' withdrawals are too

Fig. 3.1 Latest balance sheet

Assets	Printing Machine	£ 9,100	
	Fixtures and Fittings	£ 3,900	
			£13,000
	Debtors	£19,300	
	Stock and work in progress	£18,600	
		£37,900	
Liabilities	Trade Creditors	£24,900	
	Other Creditors	£ 4,700	
	Bank	£ 6,600	
		£36,200	
	Net current assets		£ 1,700
			£14,700
Financed by	Share Capital		£ 5,000
	Profit and Loss Account		£ 9,700
			£14,700
Profit & Loss Extract	Sales	£130,000	
	Gross Profit	£ 45,000	
	Net Profit	£ 5,000	
	After Directors' Withdrawals	£ 14,000	

high. This may or may not be the picture presented to you, but what is important is that you have considered and understood the position and know where you are starting from. Your prospective lender will have that much more confidence in you if you can convince him that you have a real understanding of your proposals.

Having satisfied yourself on the general standing of the business you are looking at, or the industry as a whole, consider what the future holds for you.

Let's assume in our example that you envisage three main changes:

1. You anticipate increasing turnover by 100%
2. To do so you must take on one additional employee, at say £10,000 p.a.
3. You want to increase turnover. You have found one possible major client, but need to cut your gross profit margin to 25% to become the most competitive quote.

Firstly, let's look at the costing side and the break-even calculations.

Break-Even Turnover Level

$$\frac{\text{Overheads x 100}}{\text{Gross Profit Margin}}$$

There are bound to be some extra overhead costs, in addition to the extra employee, if the business is going to work twice as hard. Electricity, lighting perhaps, extra postage, inflation — all may swell this figure.

All you can do is make an estimate, let's say an extra £5,000. The projected overheads figure will be:

	£40,000	(Gross Profit less Net Profit)
plus	£ 5,000	(to cover extras and inflation)
plus	£10,000	(new employee)
	£55,000	

$$\frac{\text{£55,000 x 100}}{30} = \text{£183,333}$$

So, providing you achieve £184,000 of turnover you should not make a loss. You are *aiming* for £260,000. If all goes according to plan, you should be profitable.

Break-Even Profit Margin

$$\frac{\text{Overheads x 100}}{\text{Sales}}$$

On the same basis:

$$\frac{£55{,}000 \times 100}{£260{,}000} = 21.15\%$$

So you *can* afford to drop your gross profit margins to 21.15% and still achieve your projected turnover. So long as this exceeds £260,000, as you hope, then you should again not make a loss.

Putting these two together you hope to realise:

£260,000 of sales
25% gross profit margin

and, if you do, you will succeed.

In accepting this fact your lender will want to be assured that your two projections here are realistic.

Firstly, the turnover: are you *really* sure you can double the performance? Confirmation of strong interest, if not firm orders, will help, but this should not be a pipedream figure. It is in your *own* interest to keep a clear head. Dreams only lead to disaster and brainstorms to bankruptcy!

Secondly, the Gross Profit margin figure. You know from your research that the norm for this industry is 36%. A drop to 25%, as you propose, should indeed be attractive; hopefully the competition would be unlikely to force you below 21.15%.

Remember, too, that we have worked these out on the basis that directors' withdrawals will remain at £14,000.

VIABILITY — PROFIT FORECASTING

You should have a fair idea of the viability now from your break-even calculations. Your prospective lender will also be getting the feel of things.

He will want to be assured, though, as indeed you will, that a profit will be generated and that such profit will be adequate:

- to ensure the growth of the business
- to cover any unforeseen revenue expenditure
- to cover any interest on bank borrowings

Now, draw up a Projected Profit Forecast along the lines shown in Chapter 2. We can draw a brief forecast up as follows:

Projected Sales	£260,000
Gross Profit Margin of 25% gives Gross Profit	£ 65,000
Less Projected Overheads	£ 55,000
Projected Net Profit	£ 10,000

Again — remember that within the overheads figure is £14,000 of directors' withdrawals. You may not feel that this is enough for all the hard work you intend to invest in the project. But even if you do, because you have been willing to reduce the gross margin so much your net profit margin — at 3.8% — shows no improvement at all on the existing pattern.

This may sow a seed of doubt in the lender's mind. Indeed, it may make you think again yourself.

The picture you create in your own situation may be completely different — but it is vital that you have a full grasp of the position when putting your case before the lender.

In our example, then, we now expect to have £10,000 profit to play with. This must be sufficient to cover any interest on your borrowing needs, as well as any unforeseen revenue expenditures.

"It keeps the overheads down."

ADEQUACY, REPAYMENT, CASH FLOW FORECASTING

So, how much do we want to borrow?

In simple terms, is it not fair to say that, if turnover is projected to increase by 100%, the overdraft requirement too will need to be increased from its present level, £6,600 in the latest Balance Sheet to double, say £13,000?

But a straightforward calculation and a few minutes' reflection may make you think again.

As a rough guide we can do a **projected funds flow forecast** to estimate the position in, say, twelve months' time. However, a much clearer picture of what will happen to your cash movements will only be evident from a full **monthly cash flow forecast** along the lines of Fig. 2.3.

Firstly let's look at the rough forecast for twelve months hence. Consider where cash will come *from*, and where cash will go *to*. The difference will be a rough indication of how you will stand at the end of the period.

Remember, though, that just because you are making a profit on paper doesn't necessarily mean that you will be any better cashwise. After all, look what happens in our example. If we accept that to double our turnover we must double the trading assets and liabilities, then:

Debtors will stand at	£38,600
Stock and W.I.P. will stand at	£37,200
	£75,800

which will be funded by	
Trade Creditors standing at	£49,800
Leaving to be found from elsewhere	**£26,000**
	£75,800

The 'other creditors' of £4,700 will help, but these are probably made up of items such as 'Rates' and cannot be doubled.

Even allowing for these, you would still be looking for £21,300 to be found from elsewhere.

This calculation is called a **Working Capital Adjustment**. Here it shows that, if you are to achieve your £260,000 turnover, and do not renegotiate your credit and debtor terms, then out of somewhere you have to find an extra £21,300 to fund the exercise in the first place.

Where can we see this money coming from then? In this case there will be two main sources:

- the £10,000 profit which we have forecast, leaving a shortfall of £11,300 which (unless you can arrange any other sources of cash) will be funded from:
- the overdraft — £11,300 and not the £13,000 we first thought.

There may well be other capital expenditures you need to make, say a new printing machine to cope with the increased sales.

Let's suppose that you propose to spend or invest £9,000 of the £10,000 projected profit on such a machine. Then your calculations would appear:

Sources of Cash	
Pre-tax profit — from your profit forecast and before any depreciation — which is a non-cash item, i.e. no cash physically to be paid out	£10,000
Applications of Cash	
Purchase of new machine	£ 9,000
	£ 1,000
Working Capital Adjustment	
Funding of £21,300 required which, after allowing for existing borrowing of £6,600, leaves an *additional* need of:	£14,700
Therefore, *additional* total funding needed after taking into account projected profit, purchases and extra trading finance	£13,700

Remember, though, that this is *extra* to the existing £6,600. An overdraft of £20,300 would be needed, as opposed to the £13,000 we first estimated — all this notwithstanding your projected profit of £10,000.

Your own situation may look better than this, but even so we should not despair with our example!

Even though the overdraft has increased the net worth of the business will have improved too, because:

- there will be an extra fixed asset of £9,000
- current assets will increase by £1,000

leaving 'shareholders funds' commensurately inflated.

Remember, though, this increased worth will be eroded by any **depreciation** adjustment needed to reflect the reducing value of the fixed assets.

And don't forget that there will be *interest to pay on the overdraft*. Depending upon the level of Base Rate this may bite quite frighteningly first into your profit margins, then into your profit, and in turn your cashflow, which would probably necessitate *another* increase in the overdraft.

It is vital that you appreciate the implications of self-perpetuating patterns like this.

There is plenty you can do to improve the position and by sensible planning and discussion you may very well turn a potential liquidity failure into a good little business. But how?

For example you could:

- improve your **stock control**, keeping stock down, and hence reduce the extra cash channelled to the provision of 'double' stock to match 'double' turnover.
- similarly, improve your **debtor collection** system, again reducing the amount of additional cash tied up.
- negotiate **improved credit terms** from your own suppliers which would effectively leave you with more immediate cash to play with.

Reducing use of the overdraft will, of course, reduce the interest burden and so improve profits.

A further solution would be to fund the new machine on a medium-term loan, leaving the overdraft to fluctuate with trading more realistically.

The renegotiation or reassessment of credit, debtor and stock control arrangements is therefore particularly vital; to see how the payment habits will affect your cashflow month by month you need to complete the **Monthly Cashflow Forecast.**

Whilst this is really a simple extension of your full year projection, it does have the benefit of identifying any *monthly* variations. But do remember that there may still be *weekly* pressures which are not immediately evident.

Using the standard Cashflow Forecast introduced in Chapter 2, amounts should be entered in the month when you expect to pay, or receive, funds.

For the sake of clarity, let's say that the additional £130,000 of turnover is to be made up of four large contracts of £32,500 in months 2, 3, 8, and 9. We'll assume the remaining £13,000 to be fairly evenly spread. Figures quoted exclude VAT.

Our Overheads figure of £55,000 comprises:

Salaries & N.I.	£30,000
Rent/Rates	£ 4,200
Directors	£14,000
Lighting/Heating etc.	£ 4,400
Sundry Overheads	£ 2,400
	£55,000

Additionally, the new machine purchase of £9,000 is to go ahead in month 2 and, initially, will not be taken on Loan Account.

Figure 3.2 (p. 44) shows how the monthly picture will appear. Remember, a credit period of slightly under two months is usual; we will anticipate payment of both debtors and creditors at 60 days, but we will need to buy the materials for contracts one month *before* delivery of the goods.

Let's look at Fig. 3.2, and reconcile the forecast to make sure nothing has gone wrong:

Projected Profit			£10,000	
Less	Capital Purchase	£9,000		
	Bank Charges, say	£2,000	£11,000	
	Cash worse off by		£ 1,000	
	Opening Bank balance		£ 6,600	debit
	Closing Cash balance		£ 7,600	debit

. . . which agrees with our forecast.

One item which requires a word of explanation before we look at the picture painted by the cashflow is that of **Value Added Tax** (VAT). This often frightens the new businessman, but it is really very simple.

In our example, when funds are received from debtors, an additional 15% is added for VAT. When payments are made to creditors, 15% is again added. Each three months, when the VAT return is completed, an adjustment is made either to *pay to* the Inland Revenue, or *receive from* them by way of rebate, the difference between the VAT received and the VAT paid.

The VAT calculation, in isolation, would therefore appear:

Sales income for 1st quarter	£32,500.00	
VAT at 15% received		£ 4,875.00
Purchases payments for 1st quarter	£48,750.00	
VAT at 15% paid		£ 7,312.50
Therefore, *Refund* for 1st quarter		£ 2,437.50
Sales income for 2nd quarter	£97,500.00	
VAT at 15% received		£14,625.00
Purchases payments for 2nd quarter	£48,750.00	
VAT at 15% paid		£ 7,312.50
Therefore *Payment* for 2nd quarter		£ 7,312.50

Fig. 3.2

Cashflow Forecast For

name of company, firm etc

Enter month		1	2	3	4	5
Receipts						
Sales – Cash						
Sales – Debtors		11000	11000	10500	43500	43500
Loans						
Other receipts	VAT	1650	1650	1575	6525	6525
A Total receipts		12650	12650	12075	50025	50025
Payments						
Cash purchases						
To creditors		81	8125	32500	32500	8125
Wages and salaries (net)	PLUS VAT	'218	1219	4875	4875	1219
PAYE/NIC		00	2500	2500	2500	2500
Capital items (NET OF VAT)			9000			
Rent/rates		350	350	350	350	350
Services – LIGHT/HEAT		365	365	365	365	365
HP/leasing repayments						
Bank/finance charges (SAY)				500		
Loan repayments						
DIRECTOR'S SALARY		1175	1175	1175	1175	1175
SUNDRY ITEMS		200	200	200	200	200
VAT (net)				(2437)		
Corporation tax, etc						
Dividend						
B Total payments		13933	22934	40028	41965	13965
Opening bank balance						
Add to B if overdrawn Subtract from B if credit	(SAY)	(6600)	(7833)	(18167)	(46120)	(38060)
C Total		20533	30817	58195	88085	51994
D Closing bank balance (Difference between A&C)		(7883)	(18167)	(46120)	(38060)	(1969)

For the period

'YOUR COMPANY' From MONTH 1 To MONTH 12

6	7	8	9	10	11	12	TOTAL
10500	11000	11000	10500	43500	43500	10500	260000
1575	1650	1650	1575	6525	6525	1575	39000
12075	12650	12650	12075	50025	50025	12075	299000
8125	8125	8125	32500	32500	8125	8125	195000
1219	1218	1219	4875	4875	1219	1219	29250
2500	2500	2500	2500	2500	2500	2500	30000
							9000
350	350	350	350	350	350	350	4200
365	365	365	365	365	365	385	4400
500			500			500	2000
1175	1175	1175	1175	1175	1175	1075	14000
200	200	200	200	200	200	200	2400
7312			(2437)			7312	9750
21746	13923	13934	40028	41965	13934	21666	300000
(1969)	(11640)	(12923)	(14207)	(42160)	(34100)	1991	
23715	25573	26857	54235	84125	48034	19675	
(11640)	(12923)	(14207)	(42160)	(34100)	1991	(7600)	

The 3rd quarter is the same as the 1st quarter, and the 4th quarter is the same as the 2nd quarter.

Aside from this, the completion of the Cashflow is relatively straightforward. So what is our example telling us?

The bottom line indicates the end of month bank requirement, assuming all goes to plan. We had estimated an overdraft need of around £20,000 on our rough twelve months' forecast, but the more detailed monthly cashflow now suggests that a facility of around £46,000 is likely to be nearer the mark! At the end of the twelve-month period, of course, we should be back at the level which had been anticipated, but the interim need must be understood.

The reason for this hiccup is quite simple. The need to buy stock in readiness for our big contracts, and to pay for these goods a month before receiving cash from sales, gives rise to a fair overdraft need; this is heightened by the capital purchase in month 2.

From this example, the value of a full monthly cashflow forecast is self-evident. Without it we would have asked the bank for a facility of say £20,000, and by month 3 would be needing £26,000-plus *in excess* of that limit, with the serious likelihood of returned cheques.

On the other hand, a properly prepared business plan, along these lines, based on an understanding of your real needs, would satisfy the lender. Providing the reality broadly matches the plan, then there should be few problems.

The important thing is to understand exactly what will happen within your business, and to keep the prospective lender fully in the picture.

ALL THE FACTS

No matter how much borrowers are encouraged to be totally honest with their potential lenders, there are always those who prefer to treat their lender as a competitor rather than a companion.

'. . . But you never *asked* me . . .' will not satisfy a disgruntled financier. You should not have needed asking.

Remember:

- Be honest, and if anything over-cautious.
- Do not hide detail and facts.

Failure to do so will only cause problems and create unnecessary friction. At the end of the day *you* will be the loser.

Customer: 'I'll be quite frank with you — sales just haven't been up to the mark.'
Banker: 'At least you've been monitoring it! Now, let's see how we can help . . .'

CONTINGENCY PLANS

We've looked so far at what will happen if all goes well.

One of the easiest ways by which a lender declines a requested facility, without directly saying 'No', is by getting you to think again, and possibly even withdraw your request.

'What if . . . the sales don't materialise?'

'What if . . . your main customer goes out of business?'

To be fully prepared, and indeed for your own benefit, you *must* think pessimistically for a while.

Write down a list of all the things that *could* go wrong. Be ready to dispel any worries the lender may have. Should the worst come to the worst be ready to react quickly with your Contingency Plans. More about this later when we consider 'A Positive Approach'.

WHY SHOULD HE LEND?

Well, we've put together the full package now. We know:

- How much profit is anticipated
- How much borrowing is likely to be needed
- How the account is likely to operate
- What the break-even points are
- What performance you would expect from this sort of business.

In essence both you and your prospective lender now know whether your project is likely to work. He can now base his decision on viability grounds.

Satisfied on this aspect he will now have to consider:

- How much he will charge, i.e. the interest rate
- Whether security is appropriate and, if so, what is available.

For a borrowing of this type you should anticipate a rate of around 3% above base rate, plus an arrangement fee of around £200.

So far as security is concerned, there is little in your greeting card business to be of real interest as collateral. The lender would be looking for Directors' guarantees backed, if possible, by a charge over personal assets such as your house.

Provided security is available, provided the project looks viable and profitable and, although reliance on the overdraft will be heavy at times, the year-on position is quite acceptable:

'Yes, Mr Borrower, this all looks pretty well set out now. I'm delighted to confirm that we shall be very pleased to assist you.'

ALTERNATIVE FINANCE

It is important always to consider alternative options. Some may be cheaper, others more appropriate to your purpose and cashflow needs.

In our greeting card example, we considered the funding of the printing machine on a medium term loan (see Chapter 4). This would have left the account operating in credit for part of the time. It would have been sensible to consider purchasing the machine over its working life, in which case a loan would be appropriate.

So far as the *trading* need was concerned, the increased level of turnover, involving the payment for goods before funds from their sale were received, left a fairly heavy, albeit short term, overdraft requirement.

Consider any cheaper options. Changed creditor or debtor terms could alleviate the pressure on you. Alternatively, factoring may be appropriate. Certainly if no security is available, a factoring agreement may fit the bill (see Chapter 6).

BE PREPARED

You should now be ready with all the answers. Be prepared to deal with any questions, and explain any peculiarities of your business. If all aspects can be dealt with at the one meeting, then you can expect a quick and positive response.

Ensure you have considered everything in the following Checklist:

CHECKLIST — BE PREPARED
● Do you look right? ● Think of the lender — copies of relevant papers ready for him? ● Thought about the right type of finance and alternatives? ● Price realistic? Worst scenario/best scenario? Break-even calculations? ● Profit forecast? ● Funds Flow Forecast? ● Full Monthly cashflow? Amount required? ● All the facts — nothing withheld? ● Contingency plans? Worst scenario? ● Available security? ● Anticipate the fee — ready to negotiate? ● Any last minute thoughts?

4 Presenting Your Case: Longer Term Finance

We have already discussed the sense of matching the life of an asset with the term of repayment; we have noted the difference between trading finance provided by way of overdraft, and fixed asset funding provided by way of loan.

This Chapter concentrates upon developing an approach in obtaining support for fixed asset purchases and projects.

CHOICE OF FINANCE

There is no reason why a capital item, or fixed asset, cannot be funded from cashflow, so long as you are liquid enough for trading not to be adversely affected.

You need to assess how much profit you could generate from using this 'surplus' cash for additional trading, and whether it would be enough to cover the costs of your asset purchase on loan.

If the loan will cost you more than the cash can generate, then it would be cost-effective to buy from cashflow.

If, on the other hand, your net profit margin would be greater than the interest rate, then it would be better to opt for a loan to buy the machine. Assuming you choose to make use of a loan you have to decide firstly whether the facility should be:

- fixed interest (i.e. structured), or
- variable rate

and, secondly, what term you feel is appropriate. This will be influenced by the working life of the asset, and the period over which repayment is viable. You will need to justify this in your budgets and projections.

We looked in Chapter 1 at the pros and cons of structured and variable borrowing. Consider which is most appropriate for you, bearing in mind:

— the current levels of interest rates
— the market's views of future interest trends
— whether you wish to lock yourself into fixed monthly repayments
— whether you are content to ride out any rises or falls of interest rates
— the relevance of capital repayment holidays in terms of your cashflow.

Having ordered these thoughts in your mind, and chosen the most suitable *method* of funding, you can now concentrate on the precise details of the *purpose* to consider any peculiarities which may demand extra attention.

The following situations should cover most business eventualities.

PURCHASE OF A CAPITAL ASSET

The rules discussed in Chapter 2 hold good here, but your prospective lender will also want to be assured of, or receive clarification on, these extra points which, for your own good, you should give some thought to:

- **Will the asset be new, or a replacement?**
  If a replacement item, then is the old one saleable? What's its value, and can the sale proceeds be used towards the new asset?
- **What will be the useful life of the asset?**
  This should be the basis of your repayment structuring.
- **Will there be additional running costs?**
  Will you need to recruit additional trained staff, or will the automation enable you to reduce your staffing costs?
- **Will trading volumes increase?**
  Have you adequate working capital, or liquidity, to carry this, or will you need overdraft facilities?
- **What will the new gearing position be?**
  As new borrowing is being taken, whilst the capital base remains unchanged, there will be inevitably a gearing deterioration — the important point is will the adjustment leave the situation acceptable?
- **Is the new asset marketable, or is it specialised?**
  Will the bank be able to attach a value to it for security purposes?
- **What is the current state of your industry?**
  What are the future prospects?

All these points will have to be considered as well as the usual viability budgets being proved.

ADVANCES FOR BUILDERS

These are often the most problematic types of lendings because of a simple conflict.

For you, the builder, it is cheaper to lay all the foundations at the same time. You want to do all the bricklaying at one time, plumbing, plastering, electrical fittings, whilst you have sub-contractors on site.

The lender, though, will always wish to be happy on:

- Security
- Gearing
- Repayment

Security

The value of a completed house is obviously greater than a partially built one, and very much more marketable. The lender will therefore be looking for the builder to concentrate upon a few houses at a time, i.e. a phased development.

Gearing

Building is expensive and demands a fairly high level of borrowing. If the full costs of a development were advanced in one go, the likelihood is that the lender's contribution would far outweigh the builder's capital. The gearing would then be totally unacceptable. This can be overcome by lending for a few houses at a time — a phased development again. Say three houses at a time are funded, and once completed they are sold progressively. Then the profit — either all of it or a proportion of it — will reduce the financing need and hence keep gearing in perspective.

Repayment

The lender will not wish to rely upon the sale of the last house for his ultimate repayment. Why should he? This should be the builder's profit, and to some extent is his gamble. Again, a phased development will be encouraged. The lender will be looking for sufficient profit to have been generated by the end of the penultimate stage for the final stage to be funded from profits. If at all possible, he will want this without the need for outside finance.

The Hare: 'Business is fantastic — I've got eight developments on the go now! I can't understand why the bank manager is so worried.'

Tortoise: 'Mine's not worried. I've only got two on the go, but we *both* know they are sound propositions. *He* phones *me* up to ask if he can lend!'

The illustration at the end of this section demonstrates the ideal formula and also takes into account these further thoughts:

- How **marketable** will the new houses be? Your lender will need reassuring that there will be no problems selling them.
- Saleability will be enhanced if you are able to issue **NHBC certificates**.
- Will there be any other **facilities** required such as performance bonds for the making of roads, or retentions held back by Councils for work to be undertaken?
- The **Standard Amounts** — as a guide — which bankers look to advance towards building advances:
  50% of the land costs
  66⅔% of the development costs
- The way the advance is made, and controlled is usually against the presentation of **Architect's Certificates** split into the following stages:
  Foundations
  Walls
  Roof
  Finishing
  But this is by no means a hard-and-fast rule, and the lender will usually be happy to fall in with your arrangements, so long as the security, gearing and repayment aspects are acceptable.
- Your lender will generally wish to monitor how the building is progressing. In fact, he will often maintain a chart and actually visit the site. This is quite normal and you need not be suspicious of his motives. He is genuinely interested. Be ready to show him what you have achieved.

The illustration in Fig. 4.1 demonstrates how you should be looking to present your case to satisfy the lender's ground rules.

Your Thoughts

You will want to structure your programme to make the most of economies of scale. For example, it would probably be cheaper for all plastering to be done at one time. Similarly all electrical work and plumbing, whilst the appropriate workers are on site. As a result you will probably be looking to do the full development in one go.

Fig. 4.1 Example

Take for example a development of six houses, the cost of each one being:

Land	£10,000
Foundations	£15,000
Plate (or walls)	£15,000
Roof	£15,000
Finish	£15,000
	£70,000
Plus legal costs	£ 5,000
Total cost per house	£75,000

You have £75,000 available and estimate that each house will sell for £95,000.

Lender's Thoughts

Before considering the proposition in depth, he will be looking to satisfy the following ground rules:

(a) Normally he would not wish to lend more than:
half the cost of the land
two-thirds the cost of development

(b) Monies to be released in stages against architect's certificates.

(c) Gearing is likely to be more than the usual 1.1, but so long as it's 'reasonable', then this should not detract too much.

(d) Full repayment preferably not reliant on the sale of the last house. This often will be the one that sticks — perhaps a house in the worst position with a small plot. The lender will see this as the developer's risk, not his.

(e) Finance for the development should not be allowed to get out of hand. A development of several 'batches' rather than one large project is much easier to control.

(f) The security position should be acceptable. The lender will obviously accept that at some stages he will be relying on partly built houses, but he will wish to minimise this — preferably again by building a few houses at a time. He will then have the benefit of built houses to fall back on.

Let's look at the acceptability of your proposed development on two bases:

- All six houses in one go.
- Two batches each of three houses.

Six Houses

The workings would be as follows:

Costs

Land	£ 60,000
Foundations	£ 90,000
Plate	£ 90,000
Roof	£ 90,000
Finish	£ 90,000
Total (legals to be paid at the end)	£420,000
To come from You	£ 75,000
To come from Lender	£345,000
	£420,000

Profit

Net sales	£540,000
Less Costs	£420,000
	£120,000

The profit side looks fine. But consider these points:

(a) the lender would not wish to lend more than half land costs, and two-thirds of development costs, i.e.

£ 30,000
£240,000
£270,000 (he is asked for £345,000.)

(b) release of monies against architect's certificates — this can be done without any problems.

(c) gearing would be £75,000:£345,000 (about 4½:1). Quite unacceptable!

(d) repayment may be delayed until the sale of the last house, unless control is particularly good.

(e) the financing could easily get out of hand. A facility of £420,000 without any evidence of completion, or a *specific* indication of how much is needed to achieve completion, could well be difficult to control.

(f) the security as the development progressed would comprise only partially completed houses until the very end. Failure to complete would leave the lender with a highly unsatisfactory security position; he may even be forced to find another builder to take over the work. On this basis then, the lender would not be attracted.

"How about a game of monopoly?"

If the Project is Split

Let's assume it is split into two batches of three houses, the first batch financing would look as follows:

Land	£ 30,000
Foundation	£ 45,000
Plate	£ 45,000
Roof	£ 45,000
Finish	£ 45,000
	£210,000

Profit from this batch

Net sales	£270,000	
Less costs	£210,000	
	£ 60,000	(towards batch 2.)

Notes

(a) Half land costs	£ 15,000
Two-thirds development costs	£120,000
	£135,000

This matches the amount sought from the lender — acceptable.

(b) Again, architect's certificates. Control would be no problem.

(c) Gearing would be £75,000:£135,000 — far more acceptable.

(d) Repayment would overlap into batch 2, as would be expected, but a contribution of up to £60,000 would be available.

(e) Control of the financing would be improved, particularly as lower figures would be involved.

(f) If immediate sales did not take place, at least the lender would have the comfort of a charge over completed houses. As such, financing of this batch would not be unattractive. If we look further to the second batch the position is perfectly acceptable:

Land	£ 30,000	
Foundations	£ 45,000	
Plate	£ 45,000	
Roof	£ 45,000	
Finish	£ 45,000	
	£210,000	
To come from You	£135,000	(£75,000 plus £60,000)
To come from Lender	£ 75,000	
	£210,000	

Profit from this batch

Net sales	£270,000
Less costs	£210,000
	£ 60,000

Profit for whole project

(1)	£ 60,000
(2)	£ 60,000
	£120,000

Notes

(a) Half land costs	£ 15,000
Two-thirds development costs	£120,000
	£135,000

(against which only £75,000 is now sought).

(b) Architect's certificates: control would again be a simple matter.

(c) Gearing now would be £135,000:£75,000 — less than 1:1 and perfectly acceptable.

(d) Insofar as only £75,000 would be sought, full repayment could be achieved from the sale of the fourth house. Certainly there should be no facility outstanding against the last house.

(e) Control would again be further improved as the figures are reduced.

(f) The security position improves all the time, as the availability of completed houses grows, and the amount of borrowed funds reduces.

Overall, splitting the development into two batches is fully satisfactory, whereas a single project of six houses would not be attractive.

This illustration should give you an idea of how the lender is likely to consider your approach. Whilst your profit margin may suffer a little, it is important to appreciate his perspective and look for an acceptable compromise, balancing his needs against your profit. But remember all the time that you are paying interest and commission fees to compensate the risk side, so don't give way *too* much.

Indeed this really goes for any lending arrangement.

SHOP PURCHASES

The standard criteria hold good again if you are planning to buy a retail business, but you should also think about the following points. Any lender will ask them and you will need to be ready with answers.

- **Why is the present owner selling?**
  Have local influences changed? Perhaps a local factory has closed reducing the potential market. Maybe a competing shop has recently opened up nearby. Sound out the area really thoroughly and know what you are up against.
- **What is the business really worth?**
  Are you just buying assets — the shop and the stock — or are you also buying an element of goodwill? In other words, are you paying more than the business is physically worth on the prospects of future profitability? Have you got the experience to carry on the business and capitalise upon this so-called goodwill, or will it be lost the minute you take over?
- **Is the shop freehold or leasehold?**
  It is important that you have thought this through properly. If it is leasehold, the lender won't see it as such good security.
- **What do previous balance sheets and accounts tell you?**
  Arrange for a qualified accountant to inspect them and advise you. This will be money well spent. You would not consider buying a house without a qualified surveyor's report, and the same applies perhaps even more to a business — the accountant is your business surveyor.
- **Is the business performing in line with industry as a whole?**
  Will extra staff be needed to offer both general and experienced help?
- **Will you be living in?**
  If so, the lender may well be looking to the sale of your existing home to inject your funds into the purchase.

- **Undertake the viability exercises.**
  Often, in addition to the capital purchase requirement, a working capital facility will be needed to help with trading; creditors may wish to build up a relationship with you before giving extended credit terms. If the stock is to be sold with the shop, then this should be on overdraft, with the shop finance itself on loan. As we have already discussed, there is no reason why a mix of funding should not be used.
- **Take advice.**
  As with any business in which you are instrumental, always think and take advice. Remember the need for insurance — sickness and life cover.

Be ready to answer the lender's questions (many will be common sense) but it's important that you have thought through and presented your case fully.

OFFICE/FACTORY EXTENSION

Whilst the thought of an extension may be nice, it must be viewed as a purely commercial venture. Is it *really* needed, and if so, can you afford it?

In addition to your viability and repayment calculations, your lender will have the following in mind:

1. Will extra land need to be purchased? Who from, cost? Is it freehold or leasehold and do you have planning permission? Are the builders you propose to use qualified and experienced? Have they offered a fixed-price contract, as opposed to an estimate which may increase substantially as work progresses?
2. If the project is sizeable it may be that the lender will want stage payment controls as discussed before.

"Isn't it about time we thought of an extension?"

3. How will trading be affected by the increased space? Will you also need additional facilities, equipment or machinery?
4. Does the industry as a whole offer you growth? Are the opportunities there?
5. How much are *you* contributing to the project? What will gearing look like once the facilities have been drawn? Do the viability and repayment forecasts indicate that the borrowing can be serviced and repaid over a realistic term, perhaps up to 15 years for this type of advance?

It is vital to put together a *full* package having considered *all* the points. There is no point at all in extending a factory or office if you are not going to benefit sufficiently to make it really worthwhile. It is unlikely that the value of the building on a vacant basis will increase in line with the cost of the extension — so what other benefit do you anticipate?

Similarly there is nothing to be gained by extending if you become so stretched that your trading suffers.

Think it out fully and critically. List the things that can go wrong. Are you ready to deal with such eventualities? Don't expect your lender to invest in an ill-thought-out proposition.

All too often bank managers hear, 'I don't understand it. Everything was going so well until I decided to expan

fighting off creditors!'

Whatever the type of advance — try thinking of every angle — then think again before putting your package together.

VIABILITY

The same rules as we have considered in Chapter 2 and Chapter 3 apply and should be followed.

Is your project going to be profitable once the proposed capital expenditure has been undertaken, and can you afford it?

So, what will change?

The whole purpose of investing either in any capital item, is expand business. This will normally be accompanied by an increase in turnover, and hence working capital needs. Will there be a need for more overdraft facilities? Decide now, rather than when everything has been completed.

Hopefully, your initiative will result in increased profits, which will help towards the third change which you must consider — that of higher interest charges.

Leaving aside the capital repayments — and looking only at the revenue item of interest, take full account of:

- extra interest on the loan
- extra overdraft interest

in drawing up your Profitability Forecast or Budget.

If the projected increase in profit is not enough to cover the extra interest burden, it might be wise to think again. Be ready to discuss the forecast with your lender.

Additionally, remember the gearing aspect. When you increase your borrowing (assuming you are not injecting the same amount by way of share capital, or permanent Director's loan), then the gearing figure will deteriorate. as we discussed in Chapter 2, be ready with your calculation, explanations and arguments for the crucial interview with your lender.

REPAYMENT

Again you must *prove* that repayment will be possible, with a margin for contingencies. By this stage you will have a fair indication of your projected profit figure.

We now need to go one stage further, and draw up a **Funds Flow Forecast** to take account of the new purchase, showing

- where cash will come from, and
- where cash will go to

leaving you hopefully with a surplus.

Your major sources of cash will be:

— your *new* projected profit
— Director's loan injections
— Bank loan injections
— proceeds from any anticipated sales
— other

Your major outgoings will be:

— the purchase of the new asset
— the loan repayments (adjusted for the new facilities)
— any additional working capital needed
— other

Use the same format as we looked at in Chapter 2, and be convinced yourself of your repayment ability. You will then be ready to put your case to your prospective lender with real confidence.

DON'T FOOL YOURSELF

Anyone can put together a package which looks good on paper. The secret of success is being able to translate your projections into reality.

It is vital then to be totally practical and realistic in making your case. If anything, be over-cautious. It's far better that a conservative estimate is exceeded than an optimistic one not achieved. If your ambitious pipedream fails to materialise — just as in your heart you suspected — then *you* are the loser. The lender is usually secured.

WHY SHOULD HE LEND?

What's in it for him?

Let's assume that both viability and repayment forecasts are acceptable. Now the lender will wish to consider his own security and income.

Security

The term of the facility, generally extending to several years, will encourage the lender to seek security. You must be ready to provide some worthwhile collateral. Ideally this will be a mortgage over property, but remember that the lender will attach little value to short leases. In all probability you will be asked for security — make sure you are prepared and not caught unawares.

Consider the various options looked at in Chapter 2 and be prepared to discuss them.

Income

Ensure you have thought about the cost, both in interest terms and an arrangement fee. If necessary, shop around for the best interest rate, and be ready to negotiate with your eventual chosen lender.

As a rough guide, for a viable secured facility you should expect to pay around 3% above the Bank's base rate for a variable rate loan; if you opt for a structured loan, the rate will be standard (fixed).

Most lenders will also seek an arrangement fee — probably around ½% of the sum requested. Again, this will be negotiable, and if it will ease cashflow there may be the opportunity to add it to the loan, and hence pay it over the term of the loan.

CASE STUDY

Let's look at a typical situation. Fig. 4.2 sets out your latest financial position. Of £126,000 sales, £36,000 (i.e. £3,000 per month) relates to your major customer. Let's say he has approached you offering an increase in business up to £10,000 per month, so long as you upgrade your machinery — which will cost you £25,000.

We will take for granted your standing as a customer, and look purely at the viability statements which you should be preparing for the lender. Firstly, let's take your profit forecast:

The existing turnover is £126,000. Your existing gross profit margin is running at around 35% (£39,000 on £111,600).

Fig. 4.2 Balance Sheet at last 31st March

Fixed Assets	Plant & Machinery	£ 8,200	
	Motor Vehicles	£ 3,100	
			£11,300
Current Assets	Cash/Bank	£ 5,600	
	Debtors	£24,000	
	Stock	£ 4,100	
		£33,700	
Current Liabilities	Trade Creditors	£ 8,300	
	Other Creditors	£ 7,400	
	Directors' Loans	£15,600	
		£31,300	
Net Current Assets			£ 2,400
			£13,700
Financed by	Share Capital	£ 100	
	Profit & Loss		£13,600
			£13,700

Sales for the year amounted to	£111,600
with a Gross Profit of	£ 39,000
a Net Profit of	£ 2,500
after Director's withdrawals of	£ 8,800
and depreciation of	£ 2,600

Your current records indicate turnover is now running at £126,000 per annum, and you have around £5,000 available in cash. The new turnover is projected at £210,000, and we will assume that the Gross Profit margin will continue at 35%. So the new profit picture will look like this:

Gross Profit (35% on £126,000)		£73,500
Less:		
Directors' withdrawals, say	£10,000	
Overhead expenses (up 20% on last year), say	£30,000	
Finance costs (15% on £20,000), say	£ 3,000	
Depreciation, say	£ 8,000	£51,000
Leaving a projected net profit of		£22,500

This all looks fine. But, will this be enough to cover the increased trading need, and the repayments of the loan? You need a **Projected Funds Flow Forecast**.

As you have £5,000 available, let's work on the basis of a £20,000 loan.

The Projected Funds Flow will look like this:

Sources of Cash				
Projected Profit (with a margin for error), say			£20,000	
Add back depreciation			£ 8,000	
New Loan			£20,000	
				£48,000
Applications of Cash				
Machine Purchase			£25,000	
Loan Repayments (over 5 years)			£ 4,000	
				£29,000
Extra Working Capital needed: (On the basis of 66% increase in turnover.)				
Stock	(£ 2,700)			
Debtors	(£15,800)			
Creditors	£ 5,500	(£13,000)		
You should have available an extra:		£ 6,000		
To which must be added your existing cash available		£ 5,000		
So, you should be more liquid by		£11,000		

This is even after: the extra interest; the monthly repayments; the extra trading need.

This all looks fine. The lender should be happy enough to back you, but he would still be looking for security — probably a debenture and a guarantee from the Directors.

You must also have considered what will happen if things don't go according to plan. For instance, if your major customer is lost, you will also lose £120,000 of turnover. In this case, then the effect on your viability calculations would be:

Turnover		£90,000
Gross Profit (35%)		£31,300
Less Cash Outgoings:		
Overheads	£30,000	
Directors	£10,000	
Finance Costs	£ 3,000	
Loan Repayments	£ 4,000	£47,000
Leaving a shortfall of		£15,700

You must think about the worst scenario. Are there any other customers you could use if need be? Is your major customer of good standing, and are the contracts firm? Be ready with the answers to all these questions, and encourage your lender to develop full confidence in you.

ALTERNATIVE SOURCES OF FINANCE

Whenever medium term finance is being considered, you should also bear in mind —

- Leasing
- Hire Purchase

Depending upon your profit position, the type of asset to be purchased, balance sheet dates and your finer requirements, either may be better options for you than straightforward lending. Chapter 7 considers these questions in greater depth.

BE PREPARED

Again, the secret to a smooth passage for your request for a loan lies in the proper presentation of your package.

Make sure *you* are entirely happy with everything. If there are any little nagging questions, then you are not yet ready to approach your lender. You must feel totally confident of your proposal and satisfied that you would invest your own money in the project.

Don't try to fool the lender. Be totally honest, and appreciative of his advice, even if you don't necessarily agree. Remember, you are both on the same side — the side of your business and its healthy growth.

CHECKLIST —
PRESENTING YOUR CASE FOR LONGER TERM FINANCE

- Decided on your needs?
- Considered other options?
- Will additional trading finance be needed?
- Profitability forecasts done?
- Viability forecasts done?
- Is it worth all the extra cost?
- Considered the worst scenario?
- Considered contingency plans?
- Still convinced?
- Security available?
- What interest rate and fee do you expect — ready to negotiate?
- Alternative financing considered — Leasing or Hire Purchase?
- Any nagging questions?
- Package typed up — copies for the lender?
- Finally, do you look right — appearance, track record, etc?

5
Research and Development Finance

THE VARIOUS STAGES

We have looked at the importance of choosing the right type of finance — but before doing so with Research and Development let's appreciate why the need arises, and why it is so vital to have an extensive business plan or budget.

There are several stages with any form of research or development project. They may include:

- — Idea conception
- — Prototype development
- — Market research to identify potential demand
- — Manufacture
- — Advertising/Marketing
- — Assessment of market reaction
- — Identifying needs for product amendments
- — Relaunch

Not until this last stage is there any sign of how successful your idea is likely to be. It's all a bit of a gamble and often hard to convince a conventional lender to provide either a loan or an overdraft.

A further problem often arises from failure to plan properly and recognise the financing needs from the outset.

Suppose you have £5,000 available to invest on R & D in your business. How long will it be before these funds are exhausted?

Let's assume they cover the first three stages. *You* may be convinced of the future of your idea, but who is likely to lend to you? Up to now, your project is no more than an idea — there is nothing tangible for a lender to take as security, and eventually you would be seeking 100% of the costs of manufacture, marketing, launch and so forth. Who will lend?

A proper business plan would probably have seen you in the bank manager's office right at the beginning, when you still had spare cash to inject and show your commitment. Even at that stage the traditional lender may have had reservations without any real sign of future prospects.

The Government's Small Firm Loan Guarantee Scheme (see Chapter 9) may be an acceptable source of security when you seek finance to enable your project to continue. But two problems still remain:

- Gearing
- Repayment

Gearing

We looked at this in Chapter 2, and you will remember that ideally the 'proprietor's' investment should be at least the same, if not more, than the amount of lendings.

Clearly, if all your funds have been swallowed up, and there is nothing tangible to show by way of assets — since all you have left is a researched idea — then gearing will be well out of line.

What you really need is an injection of capital to swell the 'proprietor's funds' side of the equation, rather than the lending side.

Repayment

Repayment may be even more of a problem. You can always find a way of arguing or explaining the gearing imbalance but, to effect repayment of a borrowing, you need to be making money. If all your 'Stage Three onwards' funding is by way of borrowed money, then the interest and repayment bill will be sizeable. Indeed the interest (which affects the revenue, i.e. profit-income element) may be all the difference between making a profit or a loss.

So, the lower you can keep your financing costs, the more profitable and successful you are likely to be.

CHARACTERISTICS AND BENEFITS OF EQUITY FINANCE

The idea of **equity capital** is that the new investor injects capital into the Company against which he receives some of the shares.

No repayment is made as it would be with a loan. The investor relies upon dividends just like any other shareholder, for his return. Insofar as there is no guarantee of this, equity finance is often referred to as Risk Capital. It may take the form of:

- Ordinary shares
- Deferred shares
- Redeemable shares

Whatever vehicle is used the terms will vary and be subject to negotiation at the outset.

Using Equity Finance does mean that you have to give up some of the Company's shareholding, and sometimes the investor will wish to introduce a representative into the running of the business. But there are two major benefits:

- **The repayment aspect** — or rather the absence of repayment. There may be the option to buy back the shares at some future time, but certainly in the short term — when cashflow may simply not be enough to service a traditional borrowing — there will be no repayment burden.
- **Gearing** will be substantially improved, as the funds are injected into the capital side of the equation rather than the lending side. Hence, as well as obtaining finance now, the improved position will facilitate the raising of traditional debt — say perhaps overdraft for trading purposes (see A Typical Buy-out on p. 70).

EQUITY CAPITAL SITUATIONS

What sort of situations then might you be thinking of equity-financing?

Start-Up Capital

Usually your new business will start up using your own injection as capital, plus bank finance (overdraft or loan) to help with trading.

Equity options come into play, though, if your own investment is too small to put the business on a proper footing, or would make the gearing unacceptable in relation to your overdraft requirement.

You could approach either:

- A **Venture Capital** body.
- An individual who may be able to benefit from the terms of the **Business Expansion Scheme** (see Chapter 9). Providing you are a 'qualifying trade' — most manufacturing and service industries and, as you will be, unquoted companies — then your potential investor will be able to claim tax relief on an injection of up to £40,000 p.a.

Management Buyouts

These are becoming more and more common, and involve the managers of a Company buying the business from its existing owners.

Suppose you have been paid a salary to run a business on behalf of someone who inherited it as a family-run business some years ago but who has no real interest in it. He may call in once or twice a month to see how things are going. He now has had an offer, say of £100,000, from a competitor to buy him out, and is inclined to take it.

On the other hand, you see your job at risk and would like to buy the business yourself — but, of course, cannot raise £100,000. You may be able to raise say £25,000, perhaps by a remortgage on your house or borrowing from your family — but you still need 75% of the purchase price. Equity finance would be the right avenue to follow.

Development Capital

The need for this type of support will arise if your planning has not been accurate enough, or something has happened which you had not forecast.

Perhaps you have done all the research and marketing work, and launched your product, but have now run out of cash to develop the business.

Insofar as your outside investor will have some indication of track record and potential, development capital does not carry quite as much risk as start-up and venture capital. Traditional lending may not be available on gearing and repayment grounds.

As the new investor will be 'buying' shares and looking to the future performance and profits of the business for his return, he will want to satisfy himself as to the quality of management. If he is not happy about it, he may insist, as part of the deal, to put a representative on the Board and to take part in the day-to-day running of things.

It is worth, then, taking a really critical look at yourself — your approach, your future, your past track record, and even your appearance.

Consider the points discusssed in Chapter 2, with particular emphasis on the first impressions, track record and project viability.

Would *you* wish to become involved in *his* place?

Venture Capital

This is a much 'riskier' form of investment, largely by virtue of the type of business.

If you are involved with high technology, computerisation and the like, which are subject to very volatile markets, then you should really be looking towards a 'Venture Capital' provider; he will always wish to introduce some form of management input himself.

In such high-risk industries development capital is not usually seen as appropriate.

Stock Market Listings

This method of obtaining outside finance by 'selling off' share capital can only work when you are really well established, earning substantial profits and looking for expansion funds. There are two Stock Markets:

The **Stock Exchange** which deals with Public Limited Companies and will not be relevant for small and medium-sized businesses.

The **Unlisted Securities Market** (USM) may in due course be worth looking at if your business grows to an acceptable size. There are various rules and conditions which must be recognised prior to being accepted into the USM.

- The Company must be public — a plc — with at least 10% of the shares already in public hands (perhaps via the Business Expansion Scheme).
- A prior trading record, preferably three years, should be available, although under certain conditions a 'New Venture' will be allowed entry.
- A 'general undertaking' must be provided by the Company regarding disclosure of information.

Applications must be made through an official Stockbroker who will be able to offer you advice and guidance. Your Bank Manager should be able to put you in touch with a Stockbroker.

In addition to these two, the **Third Market** launched on 26th January 1987, provides a market for some companies, which do not meet the admission requirements for a full listing on the Stock Market or the USM, to have their securities traded and raise expansion finance on a properly constituted market.

Usually, young growing companies would be typical candidates. There are no minimum size criteria, although there must be at least three UK directors, and you will need a 'sponsor' too, who will be a Member Firm of the Stock Exchange.

There are various rules and regulations and further information can be obtained from The Stock Exchange, Old Broad Street, London EC2N 1HP.

A TYPICAL BUY-OUT

After twenty years with the same Company — now at management level — you have simply had enough and want to go it alone.

You have a good track record in the Company which is involved with the timber trade, and have been known to your bank manager for many years who is quite happy with your expertise.

The problem is that you need £150,000 to get yourself going. This would be enough to buy a leasehold yard and warehouse together with initial machinery and a small capital margin.

You would also need some form of stocking facility, but have established that stock can be obtained on credit, on a sale or return basis, from suppliers already known to you.

This leaves the £150,000 start-up capital to raise towards which you can put £30,000 of family money.

Consider the avenues open to you. You could go to the bank for the balance of £120,000 but:

- The **gearing** would be quite unacceptable at 4:1.
- What **security** could you offer? Remember in Chapter 2, we discussed the worth of leaseholds as bank security — probably not that great.
- Whilst your plans may show that you can trade at a profit how likely will this be if you have to cover the **interest** on a borrowing of £120,000, plus **repayments** — say £30,000 per annum even over a ten year term?

Alternatively you could seek a portion of the £150,000 from the Bank and look elsewhere for the difference. Let's say that your track record and experience were enough to convince your bank manager that you would be an acceptable risk to £50,000. Leaving aside gearing (which is still not ideal), at this level the bank would probably be happy with a mortgage over the yard and warehouse.

You are still £70,000 short, though.

The security problem could be solved easily enough by seeking a Small Firm Loan Guarantee under the Government's Scheme (see Chapter 9) but the gearing imbalance at 4:1 and the repayment burden would still remain.

Quite simply, what is required is something to boost the capital base — something which will not be a drain on income by way of repayments — and an approach to an equity provider, any of those listed in Chapter 13. All this suggests the following package:

£10,000 in the form of Ordinary Shares
£40,000 in the form of Preference Shares
£20,000 in the form of a loan over ten years but with a two year capital holiday repayment.

The Preference Shares would be considered as capital, but since they are not ordinary shares no voting rights would be attached.

This would leave control of the business still in your hands to the tune of 75% — your £30,000 of Ordinary Shares — with 25%, the Equity Capital concern's £10,000 of Ordinary Shares.

On the gearing side, borrowing would look like this:

Bank	£50,000
Equity Company	£20,000
	£70,000

Whilst Capital would be:

Yourself	£30,000	
Equity Company	£10,000	(Ordinary)
	£40,000	(Preference)
	£80,000	

This would leave gearing acceptable at under 1:1.

The repayment side is not too onerous, and for the first two years only interest will have to be paid on the equity company's loan.

In fact the only downside feature, so far as you are concerned, is the need to give up some equity, but this is only 25%, and since you retain control, it's probably not too unpalatable.

From the equity company's point of view, they are investing in your expertise and are looking for profits from which they will receive dividends.

Overall, an acceptable and workable package from everyone's point of view.

'Didn't I used to work for you in 1981?'

PRIVATE SOURCES OF EQUITY FINANCE

The main source of private equity finance will invariably come from family money. The simple benefit with this is that control of the Company will stay in the sole hands of your family.

Outside of the immediate family, however, private individuals often have personal funds to inject into small enterprises, and the Business Enterprise Scheme has led to a growth of such funds.

The problem here is tying up the source with the need. If you are interested in this type of finance you must put out as many 'feelers' as possible — via your bank manager, accountant, or even solicitor.

Needless to say, however, you must enter into a relationship with an outsider with your eyes wide open. You will have no recourse against him or her if things go wrong; and on balance it's probably safer to stick with the traditional sources.

INSTITUTIONAL SOURCES OF EQUITY FINANCE

Chapter 13 will give you specific addresses, but broadly speaking the following institutional groups are interested in investing in small private businesses:

Pension Funds

These will in some cases be prepared to invest in the equity of promising looking businesses in need of growth capital. Understandably they have a fairly choosey selection system, but some of the sizeable nationalised industries have specific schemes geared to this type of funding. In the first place, you can obtain details from the National Association of Pension Funds.

Insurance Companies

Much like the pension funds, some of the larger insurance companies have funds which they channel into equity financing. The British Insurance Association will be able to provide you with details.

Banks

Whether merchant banks, or clearing banks, most have development subsidiaries purely to concentrate upon equity funding. You would well benefit from shopping around in this sector, as there will be a wide range of criteria applied from one provider to the next.

The merchant bank subsidiaries are usually more flexible than the clearing banks and, if you have high hopes with the intention of a possible USM listing in due course, then the merchant banks are the better avenue. On the other hand, if you prefer to keep all your financing under one roof, then you may find that the clearing banks would be better suitors.

Other Institutions

Other bodies, such as large corporate institutions, will often be ready to inject capital if they see their own function complemented by your own business. Their involvement may well suit you, but do remember that they may want to influence you more than you really want to be.

If this avenue does appeal to you, then the initiative is yours. It's up to you to approach likely companies for support.

In addition to the recognised public companies, there are also venture and equity capital companies. These are not necessarily linked to banks. Their sole function is to invest in equity propositions. Most are perfectly reputable, but again may want a greater involvement than you might wish. Certainly you should seek professional advice — your accountant, solicitor or bank manager — before you commit yourself.

One of the best known institutions — which is in fact owned largely by a mix of the London and Scottish clearing banks — is the Investors in Industry Group plc (3 i's for short) which used to be called Finance for Industry. Its offices are widespread, and its equity, lending and advisory facilities are extensive. See Chapter 13 for contact points.

You really need to research what is available here. Your bank manager or the local DTI office will be able to offer guidance. Then weigh up the pros and cons of the various sources relative to your need.

GOVERNMENT AID

Chapter 9 considers the whole spectrum of Government aid. Specific to assisting equity capital situations is the Business Expansion Scheme which, as explained in Chapter 9, encourages private investors willing to invest up to £40,000 per annum by offering tax incentives.

In addition to this, and the various employment linked and Depressed Area schemes also considered in Chapter 9, the DTI offers helpful publications intended at guiding you through the options available.

The Small Business Advisory Centres and Business in the Community Offices will also be able to help you get your ideas into perspective.

PRESENTING YOUR CASE

The same rules we looked at in earlier chapters again apply. You are, after all, simply trying to persuade someone to part with *their* money to help *you* make profits.

The only difference with equity financiers is that they are literally investing in *you*, *your* capabilities and *your* ideas. They are not seeking repayment as such; they are looking for an income from your ability to make profits.

So, what must you have in mind when putting your case together?

Firstly, again, your appearance is doubly important. With equity finance, more than any other type of funding, you are selling *yourself* to a prospective partner — and he's no doubt seen many other applicants as well.

The budgets, projections and forecasts discussed and explained in Chapter 2 and 3 are again relevant. The question of break-evens should be addressed, and market research undertaken to assess the potential demand for your product or services.

You must structure your presentation as you would wish to see it if you were in the prospective investor's shoes:

- Past history
- Concept
- Future prospects
- Your involvement
- His involvement
- Your proposals

WHY SHOULD HE INVEST?

Would *you* invest — this is always the acid test. What is in it for him? Could he achieve a better income by investing, say, in a building society, which would be very much safer and still give a pretty high yield — or are you offering a genuinely attractive proposition?

Look really critically at what you are suggesting. Forget the optimism and put on your pessimistic hat for a moment.

What are the downsides? Be honest with yourself and be ready to discuss them openly. Have answers ready, but don't hide anything. Remember, you will have to work closely with the investor and lack of honesty from the start is a sure recipe for disaster, to say nothing of your future reputation.

Once you have satisfied yourself that this is a project *you* would back, then you have a much better chance of convincing an experienced outsider.

WHO TO CONTACT

A full list of addresses is to be found in Chapter 13. Initial enquiries should be directed to your bank manager, your accountant or your solicitor.

The most appropriate vehicle can then be decided upon, and contact made with the right source, whether

— Private
— Institutional

In both trading and capital funding, we have referred to alternative methods of raising finance. The next chapters now look at these alternatives in more detail, and when they may be appropriate.

Trading finance will sometimes be replaced by factoring or invoice discounting, whilst capital funding may be dealt with by use of a leasing arrangement, or hire purchase.

The various grants and other sources of Governmental assistance are considered, with a chapter also allotted to export finance, assistance and guidance.

EQUITY FINANCE CHECKLIST
● Business plan? ● Project viability? ● Repayment a problem? ● Gearing a problem? ● Identified need for equity capital? ● Assess *precise* needs? ● Willingness to surrender equity? ● Type of investor sought — private or institutional? ● Precise vehicle chosen? ● Advice obtained — bank, accountant, solicitor? ● Package convincing? ● Approach arranged? ● Professional advice sought on investor's proposals or counter-proposals?

6
Factoring

WHAT IS FACTORING?

We have already considered the better use of creditors' and debtors' monies to help fund your trading needs.

It may be, however, that you are in no position to influence the term of credit allowed to you, nor to incentivise your debtors (which may allow your competitors to become more attractive). The only option would be to fall in line with market conditions and averages, perhaps leaving a strained, or even impossible, cash flow situation.

Factoring however allows you to use a high percentage (usually up to 80%) of your debtor monies *as soon as invoices are issued*. In effect your debtors will be paying you cash.

There are several other aspects to factoring which may provide an added attraction to you:

- Sales accounting and debtor collection. It will effectively do your book-keeping, send out invoices and statements and collect monies when due — and, if necessary, chase monies when overdue.
- Bad debt protection on all *approved* sales. A credit reference service would also be provided.

Invoice Discounting

Similar to factoring is 'invoice discounting'. This does not usually provide bad debt protection, nor does it include sales accounting.

Invoice discounting will, however, provide cash against trade debtors — usually against one or two of your large accounts — on a confidential basis.

Export Factoring is considered in Chapter 8.

THE ADVANTAGES

To assess whether factoring is for you or not, let's look at the pros and cons — firstly the pros:

The Cash Against Debtors Aspect

This will:

- *release funds* to alleviate cash flow pressure, hence reducing outside funding, whether overdraft or loans.
- obviate the need to surrender *equity*, control or even simply to provide personal security as collateral against outside funding.
- *reduce interest charges* — which must, of course, be balanced against the cost of the service.
- provide the opportunity to obtain *discounts* from early settlement of creditors.
- allow an *increased level of trade*, and hence a better opportunity to earn profits.

The Sales Accounting Side

This will:

- *release management* into more productive marketing roles.
- provide *staff savings* in the bookkeeping function.
- provide *overhead savings* — stationery, telephone, postages, premises needs.
- probably introduce a more efficient *collection system* than you already have.

Bad Debt Protection

This will:

- enable you to operate in a much *safer* atmosphere.
- leave you to concentrate on achieving good *profit margins* rather than simply concerning yourself with getting paid.
- leave your *profit and cash flow* intact — without worrying about what contingencies to provide for the inevitable bad debts.

THE DISADVANTAGES

Everything has its price: and a full factoring arrangement will usually work out more expensive than a simple overdraft.

You will be charged:

(i) **Interest** — on the same basis as a loan or overdraft, and
(ii) a **service charge** to cover the bad debt protection and the sales accounting. This will usually fall between ½% and 2½% of gross sales.

Both the interest charge and the service charge will reflect the risk involved, both as to the quality and standing of the debtors concerned, and to the quality and control within your own business.

HOW DOES FACTORING WORK?

Different factoring companies will operate in different ways, but it will generally start with an assessment of your Balance Sheet and an analysis of your debtor book — past and present.

The factoring company will then evaluate the risk element, and hence the cost of service, and also the percentage of the debtor book it is prepared to purchase — usually 70% to 80%.

This can all take up to about eight weeks before actual factoring begins — so don't leave your enquiries until the last minute.

You would forward your sales invoices to the factoring company at periodic intervals and, assuming you wish to take advantage of the 'advances' aspect, the agreed percentage of discount would be paid over to you immediately. On settlement by the debtor, the difference is then passed back to you, after deduction of the service charge.

At the end of each month the factoring company would send you:

- a statement showing your balance with the Company
- an analysis of outstanding debtors
- copies of statements sent out to your customers.

The arrangements continue on this basis with the factoring company chasing poor payers and underwriting bad debts.

There is no compulsion to take all aspects of factoring — the cost will reduce if you opt for a diluted service.

Invoice Discounting

This operates in a similar manner to the 'advances' side of factoring. But since control of invoicing and collection remains with you, your debtor is unaware of the arrangement. Additionally, any bad debts must be carried by you — in other words, the facility is 'with recourse'.

Often invoice discounting is used when one large invoice is involved, perhaps a well-established customer who is apt to take a long time to pay.

IS FACTORING FOR YOU?

Again, different factoring companies suit different target markets, but it would be unusual to see a factoring arrangement in companies with a turnover of less than £200,000 per annum.

Invoices should usually be for £100 or more, and be well spread — i.e.

comprise several names — preferably with good credit ratings. The credit period should be less than 180 days.

So far as your own Company's position is concerned, you are likely to be a typical potential user of factoring if you are ambitious, expanding, and would prefer to be out marketing rather than tied to the office looking after the paperwork.

It may be that you employ a book-keeping staff which is inefficient and costly, resulting in poor debtor control. Too much working capital may be lost in debtors and too many written-off (bad) debts.

Typical users of factoring are retail, wholesale and service companies, partnerships or sole traders. There are, in fact, few instances when it may not be an appropriate financing vehicle, but business involving part, or staged, payments, and retentions, would not suit.

Some potential users take the view that factoring is synonymous with pawnbroking, and are worried about the reaction of the customer when they discover that a factoring company is being employed. This is an unfounded worry. Factoring is a widely used, perfectly acceptable and efficient method of putting current assets to their most productive use, at the same time making use of experienced and efficient accounting facilities.

Care should be taken not to consider factoring, though, simply because your overdraft facilities have been exceeded and you are under dire pressure to find cash. You may simply be trying to put off already overdue restructuring of your financing arrangements as a whole.

Factoring is more likely to be a substitute for extra overdraft facilities when you are unable or unwilling to provide banking security. The only collateral a factoring company takes is an effective charge over your debtors.

THE BANK'S VIEWPOINT

Often your bank will be quite happy to see you use factoring in the right situation, and will in fact usually introduce you to its own factoring subsidiary.

There will be two areas to consider:

- Balance Sheet Changes
- Effect on Security

Balance Sheet Changes

These in turn may be twofold.

- If the agreement involves only the accounting element, and does not seek to use the 'advances' side, then the quality of the debtor book will improve. This will improve monitoring, collection, and to some extent the mere presence of a 'professional' debt collector will help. Such an improvement should be construed as 'strengthening' the Balance Sheet, and certainly as improving the value of 'debtors' if they form part of a security arrangement such as a mortgage debenture on your company.
- If the agreement is all embracing, then the debtor figure will be largely replaced by either 'cash' or 'owed by factoring company'. In actual liquidity terms in the Balance Sheet there is little change, but the amended structure should be understood.

Effect on Security

If the full agreement is utilised, and a mortgage debenture or simple charge over book debts is already held by the bank in support of existing bank facilities, then the bank must waive its interest in book debts in favour of the factoring company. This may or may not be acceptable to them. Certainly it will reduce the value of their security — by how much will depend upon how they have valued your debtors (considered briefly in Chapter 2).

If it *is* acceptable, then fine — but if not, the bank will be looking for either:

(a) a reduction in the facility (which may be quite feasible using a portion of the factored debts), or

(b) replacement security, possibly by way of personal assets, such as a charge over a private house.

Bear in mind though, and be ready to remind the bank if appropriate, that the waiver in favour of the factoring company only relates to the debtors factored at any one time. In other words, if for some reason — more likely with invoice discounting — only half the debtors are factored (or discounted), then the residual half still remain as security to the bank. Every case will be different, but it is important to work out how your company will be affected.

Overall, the banks are usually quite supportive of factoring initiatives. Be honest and involve the bank in your decision, and you should experience no real friction.

PRESENTING YOUR CASE FOR FACTORING

Much of the presentation side is common sense. A well presented set of books with a sound knowledge of the position — difficult clients etc., will all help in the factoring company's assessment. It will also assist with your negotiation of costs and charges. It's important, too, that you have a perception of how the arrangement will affect you, and what reaction is likely from other parties — such as the bank.

Let's look at a typical example. Let's say Mr Smith negotiated with his bank an overdraft limit of £75,000 for his Company a few months ago. Initially there were no problems, but more recently excesses (exceeding the limit) have become a regular feature.

The bank have Mr Smith's guarantee (for what it's worth) together with a debenture, and the rapid growth in sales and steady profit figures show the Company has promise. However, against the present resources base, the Bank has become a little uneasy about the new gearing which has started to happen — Mr Smith is somewhat bemused by the dilemma in which he finds himself. He has spent much of his time over the last few months in active marketing, and has in fact achieved record sales. The future was looking good; the only hiccup as far as he had been concerned was the loss of his clerical assistant — although the 'temp' supplied by the agency appears to have been doing a good job even if proving a little expensive.

A brief review of the Balance Sheet supports Mr Smith's claim of growth. However, the time he has spent out of the office, together with the loss of his established clerical assistant, has clearly had an adverse effect on the control of the sales ledger, with debtors rising from £130,000 to £170,000 in the last four months. As a result his cashflow has become strained and the possibility of bad debts may be creeping in.

A factoring agreement in this instance would appear ideal.

The customer has an evident need for all three factoring services:

- **Advances against debtors** — alleviating cashflow pressures and permitting sales expansion without adversely affecting gearing.
- **Debtor administration** — less expensive than the 'temp'. A more efficient control and collection service with benefits to cashflow.
- **Credit protection** — removing the risk of bad debts as the sales ledger expands.

The Bank would however lose the Book Debts cover for its debenture, and would presumably wish to write down the overdraft, say to £40,000, but the Company would have perhaps an additional £100,000 to fund its expansion, obtain creditors discounts, and so on.

The interest rate on the factored debts would be a bit higher than the overdraft, but this would be compensated by the flexibility of the additional finance, and the new business opportunities it would provide.

Invoice discounting may help if the debtor portfolio comprises a few large names, but would not offer the Company any control. Indeed, the Company would have to show that its own control was adequate — and such discounting would be a with recourse arrangement.

YOUR FACTORING CHECKLIST

- Assess your own situation. Are you:
  - (a) tied to the book-keeping function at the expense of expansion?
  - (b) finding it hard to control your debtors and make effective collection?
  - (c) suffering bad debts through your own inadequate control?
  - (d) short of working capital, which is preventing growth, yet have sizeable sums tied up in debtors?
- Is factoring for you? Will it solve your problems?
- Are you prepared to pay for the service? Consider quotes, and assess their cost effectiveness.
- How will your bank be affected? Have you confided in the bank manager?
- Are your books clear and well presented?
- Introduction via your bank manager is sensible.
- Ensure you know the procedure from the outset. Try to avoid teething problems — on both sides!

7
Leasing

'Leasing is all very well, but is not really the same as *owning* an asset. I like to know that all my machines and cars belong to the firm — it's much tidier.'

WHAT IS LEASING?

There has been some confusion over leasing in recent years — hardly surprising when you consider all the articles which have been published on the subject, and all the advertisements making claims of different benefits. Large businesses often have their own finance staff to analyse the facts, but smaller businesses cannot usually operate this way.

'Equipment leasing' added to the difficulty. Until 31st March 1986 it provided a particularly competitive source of finance for businesses which, because of tax losses or other reasons, were unable to take advantage of first-year capital allowances. For reasons which will be explained later, this gave leasing additional attractions which no longer exist, so that many publications printed before 1986 are out of date.

Leasing agreements can take many forms and there are no standard types. However, all forms of leasing have the same main *function* and can be covered by one definition:

> 'The renting of goods by an owner (the lessor) to a user (the lessee) for a specified period and for a specified fee without the user (the lessee) ever acquiring title to the goods.'

Leasing is based on the idea that one does not have to *own* an asset in order to enjoy the *benefit* of it. This has been readily accepted over the years in such matters as the renting of houses and, more recently, the hiring of televisions and videos. But only fairly recently has it been applied on a large scale to business activities.

There are obvious examples, of course, of businesses which have benefited from their investment in fixed assets over the years. Some businesses have made substantial capital gains from the sale of assets, or have improved the look of their balance sheets by revaluing assets. In many instances, a strong asset base has enabled a company to borrow for working capital and development purposes. But the opposite can also apply. Some firms and companies could have traded more profitably if their capital had not been tied up in plant and machinery. In many cases, indeed, the proprietors have seen these 'capital assets', often of a specialist or purpose-designed nature, actually depreciate over the years.

Quite simply, the profitability of a business lies not in the *ownership* of an asset, but rather in the *use* to which that asset is put.

Once a business appraisal has been made for some new venture, the choice of purchasing or leasing is:

- partly a matter of arithmetic
- partly a question of the availability of capital
- partly a question of whether or not there is a case for 'off balance sheet' funding.

HOW DOES LEASING WORK?

A straightforward or 'finance lease' is a purely financial arrangement under which the full capital cost of an item and the finance charges are spread over the period of the lease. Repair or maintenance agreements are normally not included in this type of lease.

On termination of the lease, the asset is sold and all or part of the sale proceeds are returned to the lessee as a refund of rentals. The burden of depreciation is therefore borne by the lessee as are maintenance and operating costs. You bear the same risks of ownership as if you had bought the asset outright.

It is this which distinguishes finance leasing from other more sophisticated agreements known as **contract hire**, discussed later.

THE MAIN FORMS OF LEASING

The main types of financial lease available are the fixed term lease, 'balloon' lease and open-ended or flexible lease.

Fixed Term Lease

This offers the facility of leasing over two distinct periods. The *first period*, known as the primary or initial period, is for a fixed term — usually a two or three year period. During the primary period full capital cost of the asset and finance charges are recovered or amortised by way of rentals. The *second period* may be of indeterminate length and usually attracts a nominal charge or peppercorn rental.

At any time after the primary period you (the lessee) may terminate the lease. The asset will then be sold either by the lessor or by you as agent for the lessor.

On termination, whether at the end of the primary period or at any time during the secondary period, all or part of the sales proceeds are then passed back to you as a refund of rentals. The amount of the refund of rentals will be agreed before the contract commences. The amount will vary among the different lessors but as a guide, it will be 95% to 100% of the sale proceeds of the asset.

If you wish to terminate the lease before the end of the primary period you may do so on payment of a settlement amount to be determined at that time. This amount will normally be the outstanding rentals less an appropriate rebate for the finance charges originally built into the rental.

Balloon Leasing

This is a popular variation of fixed term leasing. At the beginning an agreed proportion of the capital cost of the vehicle — 'the balloon' — is held back for payment until the end of the lease term. The balance-plus-finance charges are then paid over the lease term. This reduces the rentals to a lower level than those under the fixed term lease. The higher the balloon payment the lower the rentals, and vice versa.

At the end of the lease period the amount of the balloon is paid by you (the lessee) as the final rental charge. The asset is then sold and the proceeds are passed, in part or in whole, to you as a refund of rentals.

Ideally, the balloon payment and the sales proceeds refunds should equate. If the sales proceeds do not cover this final rental charge you will have to make up the difference.

Open-Ended or Flexible Lease

This operates in the same way as the fixed-term lease. The total cost of the asset plus finance charges are spread over the chosen period — which might be 2, 3 or even 4 years.

However, the lease is open-ended in the sense that you have the option to terminate at any point after a certain minimum period (usually 12 months) on payment of a predetermined settlement figure. If you decide to change the asset you will receive the sale proceeds and have to pay the predetermined settlement figure.

The acceptable lease period to you would normally be longer than the anticipated service life of the asset, with early termination being the accepted part of the agreement. The longer you make the lease term, the lower the rentals which, of course, improves your own cashflow.

Let's take a four year open-ended lease, with say, 36 predetermined settlement figures (one per month after 12 months): you can choose the best time to suit you for replacing the asset. This decision may be based on your current financial status, the state of the used asset market, or even the new asset supply situation.

Should you wish to keep the asset for longer than the full term then normally when you have paid the final lease rental and the leasing company has recovered its initial outlay, you may continue to a second period at a small peppercorn (nominal) rent.

Fig. 7.1 summarises the main differences, other than rental payments, between the three forms of finance leasing:

Fig. 7.1

FINANCE LEASING		
Fixed Term	**Open-Ended**	**Balloon**
You bear (i) Depreciation (ii) Maintenance Risks	You bear (i) Depreciation (ii) Maintenance Risks	You bear (i) Depreciation (ii) Maintenance Risks
You receive proportion of sales proceeds when sold via agent.	You receive proportion of sales proceeds when sold via agent.	You receive proportion of sales proceeds when sold via agent.
	You pay a predetermined settlement figure in event of early termination.	You pay 'balloon' at end of primary period — hopefully from sale of asset.

CONTRACT HIRE

Whilst finance leasing is essentially a method of finance, contract hire can often be used when you want to buy a motor vehicle.

Under a contract hire agreement the depreciation risk is borne by the lessor; this is substantially different from the finance lease. The lessor forecasts what the resale value of the vehicle will be at the end of the term and excludes this amount from the total capital cost. The balance plus finance charges, and any operating costs, are then spread over the lease term.

At the end of the lease the vehicle is returned to the lessor who retains the sale proceeds on disposal.

Contract hire takes two main forms:

- Contract hire with maintenance
- Contract hire without maintenance

Contract Hire With Maintenance

Variations in this form of leasing are generally found in the degree of services provided under the agreement. A major advantage therefore lies in its flexibility. An agreement can be tailor-made to suit your operating conditions.

Under this type of agreement the payment of a rental may cover you for a number of services which may include:

1. The use of the vehicle over the contracted mileage
2. The road fund licence
3. Replacement tyres
4. An agreed level of maintenance
5. A relief vehicle
6. A driver
7. Replacement batteries
8. Fleet administration services
9. Breakdown recovery
10. Insurance

On the termination of a contract hire agreement the vehicle is returned to the lessor who retains the proceeds of sale. If the vehicle sale price exceeds the forecast residual value, the lessor will keep the profit. Conversely, if the sale price is less, the lessor takes the loss. In this way, the lessor effectively bears the risk of depreciation.

It follows, therefore, that accurate forecasting of residual values is essential. The same applies to costs and other services.

On termination of the lease, if the contract mileage is exceeded, you will have to pay an excess mileage charge to compensate the lessor for additional maintenance work and a lower residual value. A damage charge should also be paid for any outstanding accident repair work or adverse vehicle condition. Clauses covering such payments will form part of your contract hire agreement.

Contract Hire Without Maintenance

Under this type of agreement depreciation is predetermined for you. You are left with the responsibility to provide maintenance to a standard acceptable to the lessor.

At the end of the term of contract the lessor then disposes of the vehicle and retains the proceeds.

As with contract hire with maintenance, you will have to pay for any excess mileage and/or outstanding accident repairs.

The same risks prevail with residual values, but obviously no maintenance charge is incurred since this would be your responsibility. But service intervals should be at least according to manufacturer's recommendations.

Fig. 7.2 summarises the differences and variations between the two contract hire agreements:

Fig. 7.2

CONTRACT HIRE	
With Maintenance	*Without Maintenance*
They bear depreciation and maintenance costs and risks.	You bear maintenance risks.
They receive sale proceeds on disposal.	They receive sale proceeds on disposal.
You may have to pay 'excess' in terms of mileage or damage.	You may have to pay 'excess' in terms of mileage or damage.

CASHFLOW DIFFERENCES AND PAYMENT PATTERNS

The following charts demonstrate the important cashflow differences between fixed term, balloon leasing and flexible/open-ended lease. All are based on a two year period.

Fig. 7.3 Example of payments for a Fixed Term Lease over a two year period

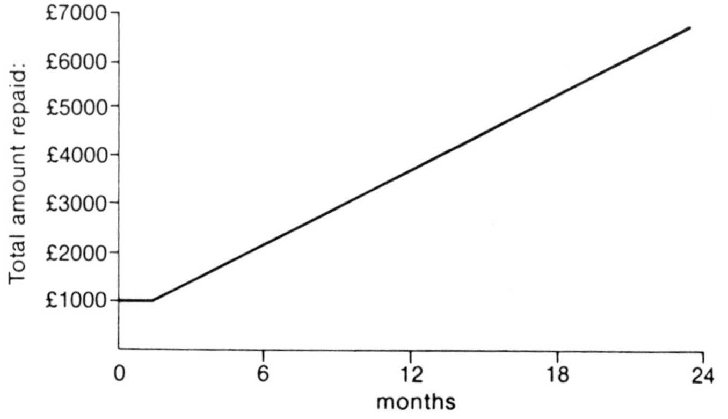

This is the sort of payment pattern you can expect for a two year fixed-term lease based on an asset costing £6,000. The full cost of the asset, plus the lease charge, is simply divided by the period of the lease in months, i.e. 24. As with the balloon lease, an initial payment of three months' rental is normally required in advance. This is followed by the remaining 21 monthly rentals starting one month after the contract date — no balloon terminal payment is required. By the 21st month all the rentals for the two year lease have been paid.

Fig. 7.4 Example of payment for a Balloon Lease

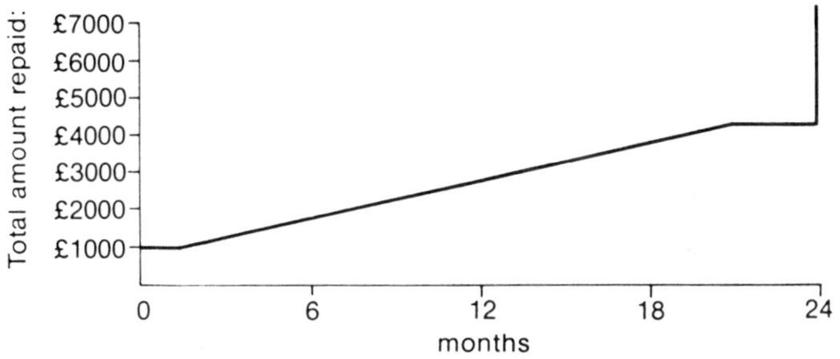

This is a typical rental payments scenario under a two-year balloon lease for an asset costing £6,000. The balloon payment is set — for example purposes — at 50% of the new asset price, i.e. in this case, £3,000. It is envisaged that when the asset is sold at the end of the lease, the sale proceeds refunded will cover the final rental payment. The other 50% of the asset's cost plus the lease charges is spread over 24 monthly rental payments, as with the other arrangements.

Normally, on a two-year lease, three montly rentals are payable in advance followed by the remaining 21 monthly rentals starting one month after the contract date and finally the balloon payment of £3,000.

Fig. 7.5 Payment example for an Open-Ended or Flexible Lease plan

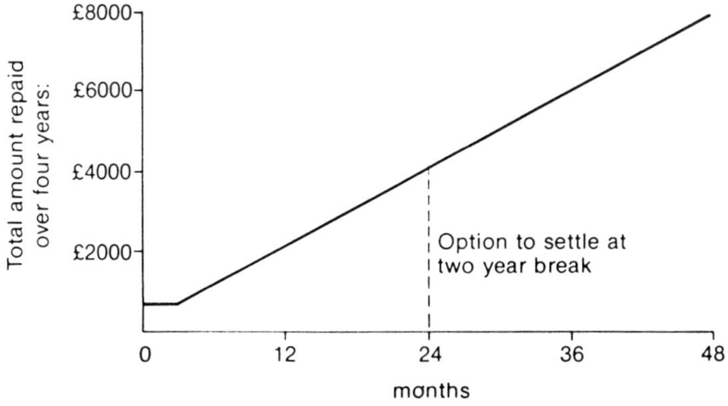

The picture is much the same as for the two-year fixed-term lease plan. However, the full cost of the asset, plus lease charges, is divided by 48 months with usually six rentals payable in advance. You also have the option to terminate the lease, say, after two years when the amount required to settle would be approximately 45% of the original cost.

On balance, from the cashflow point of view, the balloon lease over two years is more beneficial than a two-year fixed-term lease, although lease charges are higher with the former to cover the lower level of rentals.

Where cashflow is the main consideration, most leasing companies offering a flexible lease will recommend a four-year provisional lease period. This provides low monthly rentals together with the option to settle the lease to suit your own needs.

TAXATION CONSIDERATIONS

As was mentioned earlier in this chapter, the tax benefits under lease agreements have shrunk due to the phasing out of first year capital allowances in the 1984 Finance Act.

In the case of non-commercial corporations (such as local authorities and charities), however, the benefit *can* still remain. Since they make no taxable profits they have nothing to write off against in respect of the cost of the asset and its depreciation. In this case, there is a benefit to be gained leasing the asset.

As we have already noted, the leasing company itself becomes the purchaser and therefore becomes entitled to the available capital allowances (currently averaging 25%).

Assuming that the leasing company has taxable profits to take advantage of the capital allowances, the benefit of the allowances will be passed on to the lessee in the rental terms. Thus the lessee obtains indirectly the benefit of 'taxation allowances' which might not otherwise have been available to it directly.

RENTALS ALLOWABLE AGAINST TAX

The lease rentals which you pay are allowable against your taxable profits. Whilst the allowance may vary depending on the price of the asset, it can result in a significant tax deferral compared with the written down allowance claimed if the asset is not actually purchased.

Remember, though, that the tax is not saved forever; it is merely deferred. But you will have the cashflow benefit in the interim.

Another aspect you will wish to consider relates to VAT. Lease rentals are subject to VAT but this is generally recoverable by most businesses in the normal way. However, if your company involves largely VAT-exempt business, or if you are self-employed or in partnership, you should check this aspect with your accountant.

TAX ALLOWANCES — A COMPARISON

The calculations to assess whether the tax benefits would be worthwhile for you are complex. Once you believe that leasing is a possibility for you, seek further advice from your accountant.

We can take an illustration, though, if we look again at our £6,000 asset. Bought outright you would be able to offset against profits a writing down allowance of 25% of its cost for the first year, i.e. £1,500. For the second year you can offset 25% of the balance, i.e. 25% of £4,500 = £1,125.

Over the two years you can therefore offset a total allowance of £2,625. However, if you lease the asset, all the rentals paid are allowable against your taxable profits for the year in which they are paid.

For a two-year flexible lease plan the allowances are more than double those available with outright purchase. With three or four year flexible leases, as the rental payments are reduced so the allowances are reduced slightly. Even so, with a four-year flexible lease, the allowances are still 50% greater than on outright purchase, meaning a lower tax bill for the year of the lease.

When the lease is terminated and the asset sold, the refunded sale proceeds then represent taxable income, but payment of tax will have been deferred throughout the lease, leaving more cash in the business.

THE EFFECT ON YOUR BALANCE SHEET

The absence of a leased asset (and liability) from a balance sheet can in some ways present a more favourable picture to the reader of your financial statements, since it excludes an element of borrowing from your gearing calculation.

It can be quickly seen that if a business has a large amount of leased assets together with high liabilities then some provision should be made to show it in the business's financial statements.

Standard Accounting

The accountancy world is guided by various directives or Statements of Standard Accountancy Practice published from time to time. One of the most recent, SSAP 21, has been introduced to standardise the accounting treatment of leasing transactions.

Hitherto, with no mandatory UK accounting practice for leases, some companies have accounted for finance leases simply by charging to profit and loss account the rentals accruing in respect of an accounting period. The result of this is that the financial statements fail to reflect the true level of expenditure on assets which are employed in the business, and the obligations which have been entered into. Accordingly, many believe that finance leases are best reflected in the accounts of a lessee by recognising that it has the right to an asset which approximates to the rights of ownership, and that it has incurred an obligation to pay the rentals.

This can be achieved by capitalising the leases in the balance sheet. This results in the lessee recording the rights to the use of the asset as if it were a fixed asset, and reflecting the obligation to pay rentals as a liability.

Capitalisation of finance leases has been required in the United States for a number of years and with the growing importance of leases in Britain, we are now to follow suit.

In future, lessees will be required to make certain **disclosures** in the notes to the accounts for accounting periods beginning on or after the 1st July 1984. Such disclosures include the amount and maturity of commitments relating to finance leases (as if such leases were capitalised) and the amount of commitments relating to operating leases.

It can be easily seen that this is rather a complicated area and will quite rightly remain the province of accountants. But it is important to appreciate the effect of all these changes on your balance sheet, which will now show much fuller details of your involvement with leases.

YOUR LEASING CHECKLIST

- Fixed asset purchase?
- Unable to benefit from tax allowances?
- Would benefit from flexibility of leases?
- Accountant's advice?
- Appropriate type of lease?
- Introductions and quotes?
- Accountant's advice and compare quotes?
- Cost of alternatives — loan finance/cashflow funding?
- Consider Balance Sheet effects —- gearing/liquidity
- Consider 'viability' aspects and impact on profitability
- Involve accountant and bank manager in your final decision.

As with most financial vehicles your first line of enquiry should be through your accountant or bank manager, who will be able to put you in touch with an appropriate leasing company.

The overall liaison body for Leasing Companies is the Equipment Leasing Association Limited, based at 18 Upper Grosvenor Street, London, W1X 9PB (telephone 01-491 2783). They can help you with an introduction, and perhaps a local contact.

8
Finance for Exporters

FOREIGN EXCHANGE RISKS

If you are thinking of importing or exporting you will certainly need to consider the foreign exchange implications.

When agreement is reached between a buyer and seller concerning the currency of settlement for their deal, one or the other may have to buy or sell foreign currency. Indeed, if a third country's currency is involved, *both* may need to enter the foreign exchange market.

The daily turnover of the foreign exchange market runs into billions in a wide variety of currencies. Prices are dictated by supply and demand, in turn influenced by political and economic factors, and can move very rapidly.

At first glance it's a subject which can seem very confusing for those engaged in international trade, but it is important to get a good idea of the principles of foreign exchange to avoid being at a competitive disadvantage.

It is, of course, much easier for importers and exporters if they can do business in the currency of their own country. They can then establish costs and selling prices without having to enter the foreign exchange market.

However, the same will be true for the overseas buyer or supplier. He may suffer from the added disadvantage that Exchange Control regulations in his country restrict his ability to obtain foreign currency at will.

It is important to note that import licences issued by some countries do not automatically include permission for the importer to pay for goods; exporters should therefore be aware of any restrictions in the importer's country. This information can be obtained from the British Overseas Trade Board (BOTB) and the International Chamber of Commerce (ICC) — see Chapter 13 for addresses.

Sometimes, because of such problems, the buyer (or seller) will insist on using the currency of a third country rather than that of their own countries. Many Middle East countries, for example, receive oil revenue from overseas sales in American dollars.

Few exporters and importers can avoid involvement with foreign currencies as their trade grows in an increasingly competitive business environment.

There are risks, but recognising them can help the trader to reduce them substantially.

Exchange Rate Movements

The major risk you need to consider is that of exchange rate movements. These may change between the time a contract is agreed and the time, perhaps much later, when currency is received or paid. Either a profit or a loss can result from changing the currency into sterling.

If the rates move against you, such a loss could cut your profit on the deal and even wipe it out altogether.

It is therefore prudent to guard against exposure to currency movements, and various techniques are available to do this.

REMOVING THE EXCHANGE RATE RISKS

Covering Forward

Problems with fluctuating exchange rates can be avoided by getting a rate in advance, i.e. 'covering forward'. This lets you work out your profit margins accurately from the very outset.

The basis of all forward rates is the **spot rate**, in other words 'currency for immediate delivery'.

A **fixed forward** contract is for currency to be delivered to you *at a predetermined future date.*

Currency which will be delivered *during* a predetermined future period comes under a **forward option** contract.

To achieve a forward rate an adjustment is made either by *adding a discount* or *subtracting a premium* from the spot rate.

Note: The forward premium (or discount) generally reflects the arithmetical difference in interest rates for the two currencies being exchanged. It is *not* a prediction of where foreign exchange rates will be in the future.

Forward exchange quotations are generally quoted as the spot rate followed by the relevant premium or discount, from which the forward rate can be calculated.

Currency Accounts

It is possible to use a foreign currency account at your bank where there is a regular two-way flow of currency, for example where a UK exporter is receiving American dollars from abroad and also having to pay for his raw materials in American dollars.

Another way of utilising currency accounts is to borrow foreign currency now, rather than open a foreign exchange contract to hedge against a future currency receipt.

This is done by selling the borrowed currency at the spot rate for sterling immediately, and placing the sterling in an investment account to cover the interest accruing on the overdraft. The overdraft is then cleared when the currency funds are received later on.

UNDERSTANDING EXPORT TERMINOLOGY

Sending goods from one country to another, as part of a commercial transaction, can be a risky business. If the goods are lost or damaged, or if delivery does not take place for some other reason, confidence between the parties may degenerate to the point where a lawsuit is brought.

Incoterms

If when drawing up a contract, buyer and seller refer to one of the International Chamber of Commerce (ICC) **Incoterms**, they can be sure of defining their respective responsibilities simply and safely; they eliminate any chance of misunderstanding and subsequent dispute.

Since 1936 Incoterms have been frequently updated and the latest copy can be obtained from the International Chamber of Commerce. As well as the terms, it includes other definitions and a list of very useful publications. The various terms to be aware of are:

Ex-works (ex-factory, mill, plantation, warehouse etc). Seller's only responsibility is to make the goods available at his premises.

FOR/FOT Free On Rail/Free On Truck (giving a named departure point). The seller pays for delivery and has the responsibility for getting the goods to the railhead.

FAS Free Alongside Ship (giving named port of shipment). The seller's obligation is fulfilled when the goods have been placed alongside the ship on the quay, or in lighters. The buyer *must clear* the goods for export.

FOB Free On Board (giving a named port of shipment). The goods must be placed on board a ship by the seller at a port of shipment named in the sales contract. Once they cross the ship's rail all responsibility passes to the buyer.

C & F Cost and Freight (giving named port of destination). The seller pays the cost and freight necessary to get the goods to the named destination, but *not* insurance.

CIF Cost, Insurance and Freight (giving a named port of destination). This is one of the most common terms. It is similar to C & F, except that the seller must also insure the goods against loss or damage during carriage.

Ex-Ship (and named port of destination). The seller must make the goods available to the buyer on board the ship at the named destination. He must also pay the full cost, and cover the risks involved, in bringing the goods there.

Ex-Quay (duty paid — named port). The seller makes the goods available to the buyer on the quay. This will include unloading costs and could include paying all the import duties if the contact requires.

DAF Delivered at Frontier (named place of delivery at frontier). This term is normally used when goods are carried by road or rail. The seller covers all costs up to the goods arriving at the frontier, but *before* the customs border of the named country.

DDP Delivered Duty Paid (named place of destination in the country of importation). The seller pays all costs and covers all risks involved in delivering the goods to the named place in the buyer's country, which could be a factory or warehouse. This has taken over from *Franco Domicille*.

FOB Airport (named airport of departure). *Note:* The meaning of Free on Board in relation to air transport is not quite the same as with sea transport in that the word 'airport' will state where the seller's responsibility terminates, i.e. the airport — not necessarily on the plane itself.

The following terms came into force in 1980. They were designed to meet the needs of modern transport such as multi-model container transport and 'roll-on roll-off' traffic by trailers and ferries.

Free Carrier (FRC) (named point). It applies the same principle as FOB, except that the seller fulfils his obligations when he delivers the goods into the custody of the carrier at the named point. 'Carrier' means any person by whom or in whose name a contract of carriage by road, rail, sea or a combination of modes, has been made.

Freight/Carriage Paid to (DCP) (named point of destination). Like C & F this means that the seller pays the freight for the carriage of goods to the named destination. However, the risk of loss or damage passes from the seller to buyer when the goods have been delivered into the hands of the first carrier, and not at the ship's rail.

Freight/Carriage and Insurance Paid to (CIP) (named point of destination). Same as Freight Carriage Paid to, with the addition that the seller has to get transport insurance against the risk of loss or damage during carriage.

Whilst FOB and CIF were once the most common terms, changes in modes of transportation have made the last three Incoterms mentioned very popular. Importers and exporters both need to be aware of them so that contracts are fully understood.

CREDIT CONTROL

With the growth of export sales on credit terms (and even more on open account) the importance of obtaining credit information on the buyer is paramount. Many of the bigger exporting firms have their own credit control departments which use various means to obtain a picture of the buyer's payment record. The exporter's bank can use its overseas correspondent bank network to obtain status reports on potential overseas customers for the exporter's benefit.

You should also make contact with the trade associations in the various countries in which you want to do business, and so obtain details of other members' experiences. Chambers of Commerce will also be able to provide useful, if limited, information on the creditworthiness of the buyer. In some instances, various Government departments (Board of Trade, UK Trade Agency) and Embassies and Consulates based in the exporter's country can also be of help.

Over the last ten years, international credit agencies such as Dun & Bradstreet have produced comprehensive credit ratings for many companies and firms, in various countries.

It is vital that the exporter is aware of all these sources and uses them prior to arranging credit terms or arranging business on open account. Keep your enquiries up-to-date, too, as conditions can change in a relatively short period.

METHODS OF PAYMENT

This section considers the various methods of payment, from the one with the most risk to the exporter to the safest. It also looks at ways of reducing those risks.

Open Account

Goods and documents are sent by the exporter and payment made when agreed between the parties, i.e. upon receipt, at 30 or 90 days, and so on.

Risks. The exporter is in a vulnerable position because having once shipped the goods and disposed of the documents he may not receive settlement. The control of the goods is lost and any legal action must be taken in a foreign court with all its problems.

This method should only be used for undoubted first class buyers or where a strong business relationship exists. Status and trade enquiries though Banks are a necessity.

Documentary Collections

The exporter ships the goods and obtrains the necessary documentation, which he then takes to his Bank. The documents are then forwarded to the collecting Bank in the buyer's country with instructions as to how they are to be released, i.e. against payment, against acceptance of a Bill of Exchange with payment in 90 or 120 days, and so on. These instructions will be complied with by the collecting Bank; they are covered in a standard set of regulations known as *Uniform Rules for Collections* (International Chamber of Commerce publication brochure No. 332, effective 1st January 1979).

The intention of these regulations was to lessen the difficulties faced by exporters and their Banks in interpreting differences in phraseology and commercial practice worldwide.

Despite these regulations, the exporter still runs risks.

Risks. The failure of the buyer to take up or accept the documents. If this happens, the exporter will have the problem of:

(a) abandoning the consignment
(b) storing the goods
(c) reshipping back to the UK
(d) finding an alternative buyer

Very often sellers have no document of title to the goods, since they have been shipped by air, road or rail where such documents are not issued for the benefit of the exporter. Proving ownership at a later date can often be a problem.

Documentary Credits

The main problem in any trading transaction is that the buyer is anxious to receive, in good condition and before a stipulated date, the goods he has ordered, and would prefer not to pay for them until he actually receives them. On the other hand, the seller wants to ensure the goods he is selling will be paid for and, in the case of an international transaction, will receive payment before he loses control of the goods.

In certain instances he may even want an assurance of payment before he even starts producing the goods.

These problems can be eased if not solved altogether by the use of a documentary credit. In simple terms, a documentary letter of credit is: 'A written undertaking given by a Bank on behalf of the buyer to pay the seller an amount of money within a specified time, provided the seller presents documents strictly in accordance with the terms laid down in the letter of credit.'

An effort to ensure uniformity of interpretation by Banks on documentary credits was made in the International Chamber of Commerce *Uniform Customs and Practice for Documentary Credits* 1985 Revision No. 400. It sets out (in 55 articles and general provisions) the definitions, and the manner in which documentary credits will be handled for the mutual benefit and understanding of all parties.

The actual terms of the documentary credit are stipulated by the buyer when he requests his Bank to issue it. Immediately the credit is received, the exporter should ensure that full compliance with its terms can be achieved. If not, the exporter should contact the buyer requesting amendment. The exporter should make sure that all documents fully comply with the terms of the documentary credit: rejection of any of these due to discrepancies could cost money and delay payment.

There are various types of **special credits** also included in the ICC publication, such as transferable, red clause, revolving, standby and deferred payment credits. Your Bank manager, with the help of his specialised overseas departments, will be able to help you with the different credits as best befits your own requirements.

Risks. As mentioned above, subject to the exporter complying exactly with the terms of the credit, he should receive payment as specified. It is of vital importance that these are correct, since the goods will have been despatched by the time the documents are checked. If the credit is not accepted abroad, similar problems to those encountered with a documentary collection could be experienced.

Payment Upon Shipment of Goods

It is important to ensure that funds are received before the goods leave the UK. In any event, control over documents of title must be exercised before goods are released to the buyer. Make sure you receive payment by telegraphic or mail transfer just *prior* to shipment.

Payment in Advance

The safest method from the exporter's view. It means that the buyer has paid for the goods (and possibly freight and insurance as well) before the goods are received by him or his agent.

Whichever method you choose it must be fully understood by *both* parties. If it reflects a degree of risk for you then perhaps you should try and increase your profit margin.

CREDIT RISK INSURANCE

In order to protect the exporter from some of the risks mentioned, many countries now provide credit insurance.

The Berne Union is an international association of credit insurers established in 1934. It now includes ECGD (Export Credits Guarantee Department) in the UK, Hermes in West Germany, Coface in France, and others.

The insurance they offer to exporters broadly covers the following:

- Insolvency of the buyer
- Buyer's failure to pay for goods he has accepted
- Prevention of payment by general moratorium declared by buyer's country
- Government action which prevents performance of contract
- Political events and economic difficulties
- Cancellation or non-renewal of exporter's export licence
- War or other events preventing completion of contract
- Buyer's failure to take up goods not caused by breach of contract on the part of the exporter

Credit risk insurance must not be confused with marine or other transport insurance: it does not usually cover the exchange risks involved in foreign currency transactions.

"Yes, but are you a good credit risk?"

METHODS OF EXPORT FINANCE

There are many and varied types of finance available to the exporter, both from his Bank, Government organisations, finance companies, and other sources.

Unsecured Loan/Overdraft in Own Currency

Probably the simplest form of finance for the exporter and easiest to arrange, subject to Bank agreement. Remember, however, funds will be in own currency; if payment is received in a foreign currency there may be an exchange risk.

Secured Loan/Overdraft in Own Currency

If security is available, the interest rate charges on the facility may be lower thus maintaining the exporter's profit margin. Security is often by a pledge over the goods or documents to be exported.

Unsecured/Secured Loan or Overdraft in Foreign Currency

Whether the facility is taken in foreign currency will depend on the currency of the sales contract. However, do remember that currency borrowing will have to be repaid in that currency. It would be better to take this type of facility if the exporter could match his withdrawals with income, i.e. borrow in a foreign currency and convert into his own to pay for producing the goods. Repayment of the borrowing will come from the foreign currency receipts in due course.

Any exchange risk, i.e. conversion of foreign currency, would be known at the outset and could even be included in the contract price.

Advances Against Documentary Collections

Many banks will advance the exporter 80-90% of the value of documentary collections thus enabling him to receive funds immediately; the bank's security is the actual collection itself.

Negotiation/Purchase of Bills or Cheques

Many trade transactions are settled by cheque or Bill of Exchange; these require collection before funds are made available to the exporter. Banks will negotiate or purchase these items payable abroad immediately, with recourse back to the customer in the event of eventual non-payment.

Discounting of Accepted Bills of Exchange

If a Bill of Exchange has been drawn on a first-class bank under a documentary acceptance letter of credit, the exporter will be able to discount the Bill and receive its immediate face value less the discount fee.

Once again, financing costs will be known at the outset and adverse interest rate movements avoided. Because the Bill has been accepted by a first-class bank it carries little risk. It can therefore be discounted at the finest rate, often cheaper than ordinary rates.

The advances against collections, bills and accepted bills are all methods by which the exporter receives immediate cash benefit. Hence liquidity and cashflow are improved.

Acceptance Credit Facility

This must not be mistaken for a documentary acceptance credit, as the documents utilised are Accommodation Bills drawn on the exporter's bank which lends its name so that the Bill can be discounted at cheaper rates than overdrafts.

The terms of the Bills should be arranged to ensure that any trade proceeds are received in time to settle the Bills before the accommodation paper matures.

ALTERNATIVE SOURCES OF EXPORT FINANCE

The methods discussed above are all relatively short term with recourse back to the exporter and provided by his Bank.

Over the last ten years various other types of export finance have expanded and new ones appeared.

Factoring

This has been covered in some detail in Chapter 6, but suffice it to say that export factoring will:

(a) Protect the exporter against credit risk.
(b) Protect the exporter against foreign exchange rate fluctuations, enabling him to compete for business on equal terms with local suppliers.
(c) Guarantee payment on maturity of debt.
(d) Improve cashflow and make forecasting more accurate.

It can however be more expensive than many other forms of finance.

Hire Purchase

It is possible through a Credit Union to arrange for an overseas buyer to receive a hire purchase agreement from an HP company in his country. The exporter receives immediate payment and the buyer obtains deferred credit terms.

Problems which can occur are local HP regulations, exchange controls abroad, and the high cost of finance on certain occasions.

Forfaiting

This is finance for exporters — **without recourse**. Basically it is the purchase at a discount of International Trade Bills or Promissory Notes by a forfaiter.

It is medium-term credit to importers for the purchase of capital goods; the importer stretches repayment over an entire credit period, say 3 to 6 years, by issuing a series of promissory notes maturing at six monthly intervals.

Exporters receive the promissory notes which are *avalised* (guaranteed by a Bank in the importer's country).

The forfaiter then discounts these notes and the exporter receives the total sum due when the goods are shipped and documents available, less the discount fee.

The important factor here is that there is *no recourse* back to the exporter once he has received his funds.

Export Credit Finance

In Britain it was possible to obtain short term cheap finance (⅝% over bank's base rate) from banks who had the benefit of guarantees provided by the Export Credits Guarantee Department (ECGD).

However, since November 1985, the ECGD has phased out its short term schemes of up to two years, and it is therefore inappropriate to consider them now.

The banks themselves are to fill the gap in the export finance market left by ECGD's withdrawal and already Midland Bank and the National Westminster have schemes in the pipeline.

ECGD will continue to provide backing for medium (2 to 5 years) and long term finance, and also for lines of credit. All these schemes are explained in detail in ECGD's own publications which are available from either their local offices or London (see Chapter 13 for addresses).

"IOU?" "ECGD!"

DEVELOPING AN EXPORT MARKET

Developing an export market can be done in various ways. All involve a lot of market research and promotion which is explained in various publications.

Broadly speaking, the sale of goods can be carried out through outlets in the exporter's own country or outlets abroad.

Home Based Outlets

(a) *General Merchants*
Some specialise in certain types of commodity, others have retail outlets such as stores, others will sell anything anywhere for a profit.

(b) *Confirming Houses*
Some will guarantee payment by the overseas buyer, or undertake to pay on behalf of the overseas buyer. There is normally no contact between manufacturer and buyer, but the exporter will benefit from a much simplified way of selling abroad by this method.

(c) *Export Houses*
These do not normally act as agents for the foreign buyer, but buy the goods themselves. They will undertake shipping, packing, insurance and documentation and can often arrange finance.

Overseas Outlets

(a) *A Branch*
This could manufacture, assemble, sell or just give an after sales service. Care has to be taken with local taxation, transfer of profits and local laws.

(b) *Wholly owned subsidiary.*
The purchase of a going concern in the buyer's country can ease the initial establishment problems.

(c) *Subsidiary with a controlling interest.*
Prime role is the distribution and sale of parent company's products and not necessarily the subsidiary making a profit locally.

(d) *An affiliation or trade investment.*
This often helps arrange a working relationship with a well established company in the exporter's own market.

(e) *A representative or agent.*
These people can obtain orders, handle enquiries, deal with complaints, help in obtaining payment, etc. However, the type of agency will depend

on the contract drawn up between the agent and exporter; this document is very important as it lays down the agent's duties with which he must comply.

WHO TO CONTACT

Your primary contact will be your bank manager, who will be able to put you in touch with the bank's most appropriate specialised department.

Outside of immediate bank sources, you should contact the:

- local Institute of Export
- local Chamber of Commerce
- Regional or Central BOTB office
- local ECGD office

See Chapter 13 for addresses.

NEW EXPORTER CHECKLIST	
Product	**Cost**
Preparation Adaptation to local taste Adoption of metric system Packaging and presentation *Advertising* Brochures well produced Press advertising (ineffective for illiterate market) Radio and TV Translations Trade Fairs *Selling* Organisation of delivery Choice of agent Direct sales Local stocks After sales service Periodic visits by UK representative *Productive capacity* Present and potential turnover Liquid position Ability to deal with increasing export trade Outlook in home trade *vis-à-vis* overseas trade Adherence to delivery dates	*Preliminary costs* Advertising and market survey Brochures etc. Foreign travel Re-tooling? Translations *Pre-delivery* Cost of manufacture ECGD premiums Manufacturing and delivery periods *Delivery* Shipping & Forwarding Agents' expenses Marine Insurance Period of credit allowed Bank interest if bills discounted or negotiated Bank commissions *After Sales* Future visits to market Overseas staff and premises Overseas stocks Communication costs

NEW EXPORTER CHECKLIST (continued)	
Approach	**Finance**
Choice of Market	*Terms of Sale*
Small area initially	Sterling or currency
Economic conditions	Metric/Imperial measures
Area's financial and business standing	FOB, C&F, CIF
Exchange transfer risks	Overseas competition
Tariffs and quotas	Importer's offer
Patents, local standards	What can be afforded?
Market Survey	Open account
Visit by senior executive	Documentary Collections
Choice of Customer	Letters of Credit
Enquiries through:	Normal or extended credit terms
Department of Industry	*Credit Insurance*
CBI	ECGD policies:
Chamber of Commerce	comprehensive
Trade Association	specific
Banks	construction projects
Status enquiries cross checked through:	external trade
Banks	investment overseas
ECGD	*Banking Services*
Commercial sources	Shipping documents/Bills of Exchange
Visits abroad:	Collection or negotiation
Embassy arrangements	Letters of Credit
Bank letters of introduction	Guarantees and Bonds
Helpful Publications	Overdrafts or bill discounting
BOTB *Export Handbook*	Forward Exchange contracts
BOTB *Hints to Businessmen*	Export/ shipbuilding finance
Bank publications and CBI bulletins	Currency advances
	Payments abroad
	Enquiries

9
Government Grants and Assistance

A CHANGING ENVIRONMENT

Up to now we have looked purely at raising finance with a view to repayment (with the possible exception of equity finance in Chapter 5). We now turn to possible sources of grant support and incentives which may be available on beneficial terms, or even as permanent capital injections.

The political implications of supporting new business, especially in depressed and declining areas, are such that the Government has been forced to devote more and more time and resources to this field.

High unemployment has demanded attention, as have the social and ethnic problems of deprived areas such as Toxteth in Liverpool and Handsworth in Birmingham, giving rise to the creation of **Assisted Areas**.

The need to encourage the creation of small businesses has identified a market for tax and other incentives, whilst the desire to recognise the importance of New Technology offers specific support to this sector.

The economic and political climate is always changing. Schemes, incentives and grants will be introduced and modified as any Government reacts to such changes. It is important, therefore, to seek the most up-to-date information in deciding whether what is currently available will suit you.

Probably your best first contact is the nearest Department of Trade and Industry Regional Office — see Chapter 13 for addresses — but your bank manager should have a fair idea of what is likely to be appropriate in your own case; he should certainly have details of any local grants or incentives.

Broadly speaking, though, assistance falls into several categories —

- Incentives
- Geographical support
- High Technology support
- Employment linked support
- More general financial advice.

INCENTIVES

When we come to tax allowances and incentives, it cannot be emphasised enough that professional accountancy advice is vital. This need not cost the earth — look on it as a worthwhile investment — your bank manager will be able to make introductions if you need them.

The arrangements for taxation are complex and 'balance sheet year ends' may be an important factor — hence the need for the experts; but over the last few years changes have been introduced to help the small businessman, not only financially but administratively.

The 1984 Budget represented the final stage of Business Taxation Reform reducing the rates of tax on Company and Partnership profits to 30% (at the small business end) and 29% respectively. It also introduced changes relating to Capital Allowances — discussed in Chapter 7 in relation to leasing.

Successive Finance Acts have made minor amendments to the arrangements for specific sectors of industry, but there are still some major schemes you need to be aware of:

Business Expansion Scheme

The BES was introduced in 1983 to allow UK residents to invest up to £40,000 in unquoted, incorporated trading companies — on the basis of capital — and receive tax relief at their highest rate (up to 60% for top taxpayers) on the amount invested.

There are some important conditions attached. Perhaps the most relevant one is that the investor should not be too closely connected with the company — for instance, he/she must not be an employee or a paid director.

There are also some restrictions on the minimum term for which the investment must remain in the company to qualify fully — still running at 5 years after the 1986 Budget when new legislation was introduced to exempt future BES investments from Capital Gains Tax on their first disposal. Some types of business are excluded from the Scheme altogether.

BES was initially to have ceased in 1987, but it has now been confirmed as continuing indefinitely.

Information on procedure can be obtained from local Tax Offices, but effectively the investor injects funds into the company, receiving a Share Certificate. On application, the Tax Inspector will forward a Form BES 1 for the company to fill in, and once satisfied as to the background, will authorise the company to issue *Certificates of Relief* on which the tax relief is available.

As a shareholder, the investor will be eligible for dividend payments which, with the tax incentives, can give an excellent return on the investment. From the company's stance, it can be an attractive way of raising equity finance.

Small Firms Loan Guarantee Scheme

This, too, was reaffirmed in the 1986 Budget. It is aimed at companies whose business propositions stand up in all respects except the availability of security — in other words, applications to the Bank which have been declined simply because there wasn't enough security.

The scheme offers a 70% guarantee to Banks against new lending to the company; the guarantee is designed to give sufficient comfort to the bank manager to encourage him to lend.

A spin-off benefit is that banks are not permitted to take personal security — say a charge over your house — in addition to the guarantee. This may represent a good alternative to tying up your personal assets.

There is, of course, a cost for this. A 2½% premium is payable to the Government, in addition to the interest charge set by the lender (generally a preferential rate in view of the quality of the guarantee). Overall, then, the package can be very attractive — particularly as it offers repayment of up to seven years, plus the option of a two-year capital repayment holiday.

Procedurally, you should apply through the bank. If the manager is satisfied as to:

- the eligibility of your proposals
- their viability
- but will not lend due to inadequate security

then *he* will arrange for the forms — completed by yourself — to be forwarded to the Department of Trade for confirmation.

Guarantees are available for up to £75,000 and can be approved by the bank. It is very rare for the DTI to turn down an application once the bank has approved it.

The banks do have a responsibility to the Government, though, to minimise losses. Your application must be fully thought through and presented following the guidelines discussed in the first few chapters of this book.

Any queries about this scheme should initially be channelled through your bank manager, or addressed to your Regional DTI office.

GEOGRAPHICAL SUPPORT

Support for **Specific Areas** falls broadly into three categories — but all are aimed at:

- devoloping depressed areas
- bringing industry and employment to depressed or deprived areas.

The categories can be split as follows:

1. Assisted Areas
2. Rural and Tourism
3. Local Authority Aid, Enterprise Zones, Free Ports.

1. Assisted Areas

These in turn fall into:

- Intermediate Areas
- Development Areas

As economic and political environments change, different areas may be designated as Assisted Areas. Enquiry should be made of the DTI (or Scottish and Welsh Offices) for full details.

The established Areas warranting Assistance however are generally recognised as:

— Cornwall and South West Devon
— South and South West Wales
— North Wales
— Merseyside
— Humberside
— Tyneside and the North East Coast
— West Cumbria
— Northern Ireland

Within each region the Areas most in need of assistance are the **Development Areas**, with a few **Special Development Areas**. The less critical locations are the **Intermediate Areas**.

Having established whether you qualify — what is available? There are two primary types of support:

(i) *Regional Development Grants*
These are available only in Development Areas, offering grants of up to 15% (or 22% in Special Development Areas) towards Capital Purchases in specific industries (primarily in manufacturing). You must be creating, or improving, productivity and employment. In fact, instead of the 15% calculation, £3,000 per new employee can be paid.

There are various criteria and conditions laid down — so enquiry is worthwhile; applications should be directed through your nearest Regional Development Grants Office (see Chapter 13).

(ii) *Regional Selective Assistance*
This is available in any of the Assisted Areas aimed at creating or preserving employment, both within manufacturing and service projects. The amount available is by negotiation, but generally levied at the minimum necessary to ensure that the project goes ahead. Make enquiries and applications via the nearest Regional DTI office.

Additionally a special range of incentives is available for Northern Ireland and in all Assisted Areas the Government also helps by the provision of factories for rent or sale. An In-Plant Training Scheme offers up to 40% for instruction to trainees where training is essential to the success of the project.

2. Rural and Tourism

Assistance aimed at encouraging the growth of small businesses in rural areas can be obtained in:

- England, from COSIRA — the Council for Small Industries in Rural Areas
- Wales, from Welsh Development Agency, Mid-Wales Development
- Scotland, from Scottish Development Agency, or HIDB, the Highlands and Islands Development Board
- Northern Ireland, from LEDU, the Small Business Agency for Northern Ireland.

COSIRA provides advice and, in some cases, loans of up to one-third towards the cost of premises or capital items, maximum of £75,000. Repayment can be up to 20 years, with COSIRA working alongside the banks rather than in competition with them.

In Wales, the Welsh Development Agency fulfils the functions of COSIRA, and in Scotland the Scottish Development Agency. Northern Ireland is served by LEDU.

Additionally, in the Highlands of Scotland, the HIDB offers advice, support services, cheap premises and low interest loans for a wide range of purposes.

And in Mid-Wales, advice, support and cheap facilities are provided by Mid-Wales Development.

See Chapter 13 for addresses.

3. Local Authority/Enterprise Zones/Free Ports

All kinds of support may be available from different Local Authorities depending upon local policies and the needs of a particular area. Enquiry should be made of the Industrial Development Officer at your Local Authority.

In some city centres, the problems may warrant the Secretary of State designating a specific location as an **Inner Urban Area** where grants of 75% may be available in the form of Urban Development Grants.

Urban Development Corporations exist to encourage growth and development in Merseyside and the London docklands. Advice, premises and so on may be available from Development Corporations in the following designated **New Towns**:

- Bracknell
- Corby
- Crawley
- Harlow
- Hatfield
- Hemel Hempstead
- Northampton
- Redditch
- Skelmersdale
- Stevenage
- Welwyn Garden City

Again, the Welsh and Scottish Development Agencies will be able to help in several ways.

Across the country, many **Enterprise Zones** have been set up (further information from the DTI) offering exemption from rates and other benefits designed to help cashflow and reduce administrative costs and planning difficulties. Again the aim is to encourage industrial and commercial development in depressed areas.

A further Government-sponsored scheme — aimed at assisting concerns importing and re-exporting the same goods — relates to **Free Ports**; areas adjacent to specified ports are exempt from Customs and VAT regulations, providing that the imported goods are re-exported and do not pass out of the Zone. Landing, storage, shipping and repackaging are all permitted within the Free Ports, and the exemption from duties helps cashflow. Simplified procedures release some of the administrative burden, too.

The following constitute Free Ports:

- Belfast Area
- Birmingham Area
- Cardiff
- Liverpool
- Prestwick Airport
- Southampton

Enquiries should be made directly to the appropriate Free Port authority.

HIGH TECHNOLOGY SUPPORT

The major body offering support to Innovation and Technology is the SFI the Department of Trade's **Support for Innovation** programme. This provides grants of up to 33⅓% of the costs of taking a project from inception to commercial launch. It applies only to companies, but covers many areas of technology.

Applications and enquiries should be addressed to your nearest Regional DTI office.

Within the SFI scheme are several specialist programmes covering:

- Biotechnology — refer to the DTI
- Computerisation via computer-aided design, computer-aided manufacture (CADCAM) and via computer-aided design, manufacture and test (CADMAT). Refer to the Institution of Electrical Engineers, Savoy Place, London, WC2R 0BL.
- Fibre Optics and Opto-Electronics Scheme — refer to the DTI
- Flexible Manufacture Systems — refer to the DTI
- Industrial Robots — refer to the DTI
- Microelectronics Industry Support Programme — refer to the DTI
- Microelectronics Application Project — refer to the DTI
- Software Products Scheme — refer to the National Computing Centre Ltd, Oxford Road, Manchester M1 7ED.

A further body — the **British Technology Group** (BTG) — incorporates the National Research Development Corporation and the National Enterprise Board, with the aim of developing new technology. BTG fulfils essentially an equity function offering up to 50% of development funds. This is subject to a levy on future sales from which it expects to recover its investment. Further details from the BTG, Newington Causeway, London SE1 6BU.

EMPLOYMENT LINKED SUPPORT

In the last few years, unemployment has been a major political worry encouraging special attention by the Government.

Three avenues are worth exploring:

Department of Employment
Manpower Services Commission
Assisted Areas Support

Department of Employment

This offers three main schemes:

1. *Enterprise Allowance Scheme* for unemployed 18 year olds (plus) with access to £1,000 to invest in a business. It provides £40 per week (taxable) for up to one year.

2. *Job Splitting Scheme* which provides a grant of £840 to employees who split an existing full time job or aggregate overtime to form part time jobs.

3. *Job Release Schemes* — either the *full time scheme* which provides a weekly allowance to employees approaching normal state retirement age who decide to retire early hence creating a new employment situation; or the *part time scheme* which offers half the full-time scheme allowance for employees reverting to part time employment when nearing normal state pension age. Details can be obtained from Job Centres or the Department of Employment.

Manpower Services Commission

Again this offers three schemes:

1. *Management Extension Programme* which provides existing businesses with expert professional advice free of charge.

2. *Employment Transfer Scheme* affording financial encouragement for unemployed workers relocating to areas where jobs are available.

3. *Job Search Scheme* offering travel expenses for unemployed people seeking work in new areas. Job Centres will be able to provide necessary details.

Assisted Areas Support

Within these areas, which we have already discussed:

1. *Regional Selective Assistance* may be available in the form of grants for projects aimed at preserving employment.

2. *Office and Service Industries Scheme* (OSIS) provides grant support to Service industries (not manufacturers). It is based on the number of new jobs a new project will create in Assisted Areas over a three year term.

As with other Assisted Area support, applications should be directed to the DTI.

ADVISORY SERVICES

Support is not simply limited to finance; there are many bodies whose primary function is to provide advice.

Most recognised is probably the **Small Firms Service** run by the Department of Trade. It offers advice from around one hundred centres in the country — further information from the DTI.

A similar service is handled by the **Local Enterprise Agencies** run by Business in the Community from whom details can be obtained (see Chapter 13 for contacts).

We have already looked at the grants available from the Development Agencies and COSIRA, but their function as providers of advice should not be ignored. These cover the broader concept of advice to businessmen, but there are several more specific bodies:

- *Design Advisory Service Funded Consultancy Scheme* — providing a period of free consultancy in product design. Further information from the Design Council, tel: (01) 839 8000.
- *Energy Advisory Services* are available from the Energy Efficiency Office, tel: (01) 211 7156.
- *Manufacturing Advisory Service* — with similar consultancy facilities is offered by the Production Engineering Research Association (PERA), tel: (0664) 64133.

A further service, *Quality Assurance Projects* is run under the auspices of the DTI. It offers advice and grants to help small businesses towards the cost of consultants' recommendations for improving their quality assurance procedures.

FURTHER SUPPORT FOR SMALL BUSINESS

In addition to financial, employment and advisory support various **Training Schemes** exist to assist with continuing quality of work and management as new ventures develop.

The Manpower Services Commission runs several schemes and programmes aimed both at small businesses and the self-employed. For more sophisticated projects the MSC sponsors study at several Business Schools within the **New Enterprise Programme**. For MSC addresses see Chapter 13.

The **Youth Training Scheme** exists to train young school leavers for work experience. The scheme involves a package of financial and advisory support and, of course, complements the 'employment encouragement' objective. Again, the MSC is the appropriate contact point.

Training for managers of small businesses, as opposed simply to employees, is available through the **Management Extension Programme**. Courses are also run for specific skills — largely aimed at computerisation and new technology.

Fuller information regarding these facilities, which tend to change in line with Government trends, can be obtained from the MSC and the Industry Training Boards (ITBs).

EXPORT FINANCE SERVICES

We have already looked at finance for exporters in Chapter 8 and this remains a function of the Banks, not the Government.

Until recently, guarantees and insurance policies were available through the Export Credit Guarantee Department (ECGD), but these have now been modified. The individual banks are in the process of introducing their own schemes.

For financial advice on exporting, then, you should approach your bank manager.

One advisory body with Government links is the **British Overseas Trade Board (BOTB)** — sponsored by the DTI — whose members are experienced businessmen.

The main function of the BOTB is to provide advice and information, but grants and loans may be available. Further information is available from your local DTI office.

EUROPEAN FINANCE

As well as Government backing in the UK, loans and grants are available from various European sources:

European Investment Bank (EIB)

This provides loans of up to 50% of projects aimed at helping regional development, and generally furthering the work of the EEC. The terms of the loans are particularly attractive; they are generally cheaper than normal UK lending, and also allow repayment up to ten years with the option of a two-year capital repayment holiday. The DTI will have all the necessary facts.

European Regional Development Fund (ERDF)

This operates in conjunction with the DTI to help areas suffering from the loss of jobs in shipbuilding, steel and textiles. Grants of up to 70% are available.

European Coal and Steel Community (ECSC)

This offers similar sorts of facilities as the ERDF, but geared towards lost jobs in the coal and steel regions, in the form of loans. Their terms look for repayment of up to eight years and are levied at about the same level as the EIB, but rebates of up to 5% may be available depending on how many jobs are created.

European Social Fund

This offers grants aimed at training unemployed people.

Further information on all these schemes should be available from the DTI.

PREPARING YOUR CASE

Bear in mind here that you are seeking something for nothing! Insofar as the provider will often not be looking for repayment, the risk element does not demand quite so much attention, but there is a greater emphasis on justification.

It is vital, therefore, that you yourself remain convinced of the project's viability and can satisfy the provider that you have a worthwhile case.

Most only have a limited budget, and you will certainly be in competition with other applicants; if their cases are better thought out, researched and presented, they are more likely to be favoured. Remember, too, that in many instances the monies on offer will be public funds available from rates and taxes. The provider may have to satisfy an 'inspectorate body' — or auditor — as to his decision, as well as satisfying his own conscience.

Your case will, therefore, need presenting in no less detail than you would adopt going to the bank. The rules in Chapter 2 hold good here, and be ready too to answer queries and *justify* what you propose.

Contrary to 'Opposition' claims, the Government does not pour your money down the drain. Any grant you seek to receive, you should be prepared to work hard for.

WHO TO CONTACT

This will really depend upon what sort of assistance you need. Start with your bank manager; he should have first-class local knowledge of what is available. More specifically relevant addresses are given in Chapter 13.

Intermediate contact points:

- for small or new business financial grants, contact the Department of Trade and Industry's head office in London.

- for details of geographical support, contact your nearest regional office of the DTI, the Welsh Office or the Scottish Office.

- for employment-based support, contact the Department of Employment or Manpower Services Commission.

Obtaining the finance and launching your project is only the beginning: you must be constantly alive to the development of the business, the progress being made, and any slippage which may be occurring.

The final chapters look at:

— monitoring disciplines
— when things are going right
— when things are going wrong

CHECKLIST
● Researched what's available? ● Researched the criteria you must fulfil? ● Do you fit? ● Does your case stand up? Are you convinced? ● Specific benefits: — creating employment? — developing areas? — new technology? ● Projections/viability, calculations etc? ● Any likely questions — have you an answer? ● Well presented package available — copy to leave with the 'provider'? ● Do *you* look right? ● Would *you* invest your own money in the project?

10
As You Go Along

THE NEED FOR MONITORING

You must at all times be able to assess your:

- financial position
- profit progress
- liquidity
- current balance sheet strength
- value of assets for security purposes.

Failure to give proper thought to these points will mean that you will not react in the best way, both in good and bad times.

In the *good times* you must be ready to make the most of cash surpluses — either by investment or expansion. Equally, in the *bad times* you must be prepared to reverse loss-making trends as quickly as possible. To await the availability of audited accounts — often many months after the year-end — may be extremely costly and possibly too late.

You may need extra financing as the year unfolds. Any such requests will generally beg the question of, 'What is your progress to date?'

If you cannot produce this, then your presentation will be incomplete and your prospective lender will lose some confidence in you.

'I'd *like* to have helped further, but he simply didn't give me anything to go on.'
Surrey Bank Manager.

On a purely business basis, if you fail to monitor collection of debtors, the debtors will soon imagine that you give extended credit — and simply not pay until pressed. This will damage your liquidity, and your profit margins, too.

It is vital then always to *monitor* progress, and be ready to *react* to it. Don't be tempted to ignore the monitoring process — it's time consuming, and time will probably be at a premium in the early stages — but it's important.

MANAGEMENT FIGURES

So what sort of monitoring should you undertake?

You should be drawing up — preferably on a monthly basis — Management Figures, although this title covers a multitude of sins.

Really, whatever *you* need to keep tabs on your business should form part of *your* Management Accounts.

As a general rule, your major concern should centre on **liquidity**, for three reasons:

1. to assess how accurate — on an ongoing basis — your Projected Cashflow Forecast is; this will be a pointer to any changes in your need for overdraft facilities. Any lender would much prefer to be warned in advance of an impending increased need, rather than afterwards, by which time either

   - cheques have been returned or
   - unauthorised borrowing has taken place

2. to ensure that the best use is made of your **assets**, your stock and debtors should be kept to a workable minimum, and creditors to an acceptable maximum. Only by close monitoring can this be achieved. Too much cash tied up in unsaleable stock or poor paying debtors will increase your need for bank, or other outside — and expensive — financing.

3. to give quick indications of ongoing **profitability**. Put simply — in the absence of any capital purchases or capital sales, an improvement in liquidity will show profits, whilst a deterioration in liquidity shows losses.

CASHFLOW MONITORING

No one expects your Cashflow Forecast to be absolutely on target, but if there is any *wide* divergence from your projection, then you will be expected to identify this when it is happening — not six months later when both you and a rather nervous lender try to find out what went wrong.

In Chapters 2 and 3 we looked at the compilation of cashflows. A useful exercise is to draw up your projection with a 'forecast column' and an 'actual column', along the lines of Fig. 10.1.

As the months pass by, complete the actual column adjacent to the forecast column. Any material and permanent slippage should be identified and discussed with the lender as soon as possible.

Fig. 10.1 A simple way of monitoring monthly cashflow

	January		*February*		*March*	
	Forecast	Actual	Forecast	Actual		
Receipts						
Sales — Cash						
— Debtors						
Loans						
Other receipts						
Total 'Ins'						
Payments						
Cash Purchases						
Creditors						
Wages, Salaries						
PAYE/NI						
Capital Purchases						
Rent/Rates						
Services						
HP/Leasing						
Bank charges						
Loan Repayments						
Other outgoings						
V.A.T.						
Corporation Tax						
Total 'Outs'						
Opening Bank Balance						
Closing Bank Balance						

PROFIT PERFORMANCE

It's important to recognise that profit does not necessarily mean cash. Profit may be represented by an increase in stock or debtors, or perhaps by a decrease in creditors — or some combination of all three. Alternatively, it may show through in increased capital assets.

In effect, profit may be referred to as growth.

Let's assume that there have been no capital items — either purchases or sales — and concentrate purely on the liquid items in the cashflow, or balance sheet. Then in simple terms:

- an improvement in liquidity shows profitable trading
- a deterioration in liquidity shows losses.

If there have been capital movements, then an adjustment will be necessary, as it will if cash has been introduced, perhaps directors' loans or permanent cash injections.

Nonetheless, the calculation is relatively straightforward. As with the Cashflow Forecast it should be compared with your Profit Projection or Budget, with any material variance being noted.

The importance of spotting any change — particularly a fall in the profit margin — probably goes without saying. A reassessment of the whole viability exercise may be called for, and remedial action taken. If left unchecked irreparable damage may be done, and the future of your business threatened.

LIQUIDITY TRENDS

Your lender will have an extensive list of **liquidity ratios** which he will diligently work out to check the progress of your business.

These should not be seen as banker's jargon, but rather used by you to spot any changes — for instance period of credit given, or taken, or the speed at which stock is turning over.

Broadly they fall into three categories:

- Resources Trends
- Liquidity Trends
- Profitability Trends

It is quite possible to — and large companies do — spend time calculating the Resources and the Profitability Ratios to show progress with gearing and profit margins. But the main emphasis should be on the *liquidity* ones.

Those normally considered will be:

1. Current Ratio
2. Liquid Ratio
3. Stock Turnover
4. Credit Given
5. Credit Taken

1. Current Ratio

This is the relationship between your 'current assets' and your 'current liabilities' usually expressed as:

$$\frac{\text{Current Assets}}{\text{Current Liabilities}}$$

Anything over '1.0' is acceptable, since it shows that there are more assets available to meet immediate liabilities than there are immediate assets. A margin is healthy of course, and the quality of the underlying assets must be considered. Any deterioration — month by month — of this figure will need looking at.

Conversely any marked increase will also warrant enquiry, since you may not be using your assets most profitably.

But there's no need either to overreact or underreact. Some businesses do very well on a remarkably narrow margin, while others rely on a much broader cushion.

It is the *trend* which holds the key — any movement in the *trend* should be questioned.

2. Liquid Ratio

This is the same as the Current Ratio, except that it ignores stock. It takes the view that, in the worst scenario, the stock will either prove worthless, or will 'disappear with the Directors'.

The ratio offers a good indication of how easily current liabilities could be satisfied from cash and debtors alone.

Frequently this will come out at below 1.0 (which is hardly surprising) but again the important aspect is that of changing *trends*.

3. Stock Turnover

This indicates whether any dead, outdated, or defective stock is being held, or whether good stock is building up in excess of forecasts. This may be the result either of poor stock control, or difficult trading conditions both necessitating and causing stock build-ups.

The Stock Turnover ratio is expressed in days and calculated:

$$\frac{\text{Stock}}{\text{Purchases (year to date)}} \times 365$$

Once again, the trend is the important factor and any change should be investigated and explained. A useful exercise here is to compare the stock turnover figure with that for the average for your particular industry. How do you compare? If much different, you should look for first an explanation and then an improvement.

4. Credit Given

Or, how much credit are your debtors taking, or being allowed by you? Debtors are probably one of your major sources of trading finance, and — providing your terms do not become unattractive — should be minimised.

A deteriorating trend here may highlight a developing bad debt problem which would need looking at straightaway, but it may also bring to light a slippage in collection efficiency — perhaps you are too busy with other matters to chase debtors? It may be that factoring (see Chapter 6) could be the answer.

The ratio is again expressed in days:

$$\frac{\text{Debtors}}{\text{Sales (year to date)}} \times 365$$

Once more, whilst the emphasis is on trends, a comparison with your industry norm should be made.

Lenders will often look for Age Lists of your debtors and 'spread' of debtors, indicating any long outstanding debts (why?), and how many customers owe you money. Lenders prefer a wide portfolio of names.

One large debtor — if he defaulted — could cause you grave problems indeed.

It is worthwhile, then, as much for your own benefit as the lender's, to keep these lists fully up-to-date.

5. Credit Taken

This is really just the reverse of credit given. The lender will look for two points in particular here. First, the 'spread' of creditors — how many people do you owe money to, and again, if just one, what would be the effect of either pressure for payment, or withdrawal of the credit line? Second, are your preferential creditors, i.e. VAT, tax etc, up to date, or will pressure soon be brought to bear?

As with credit given, the ratio is expressed in days, and should as with the other ratios be compared with your industry norms:

$$\frac{\text{Credit Taken}}{\text{Purchases (year to date)}} \times 365$$

BALANCE SHEET ASSESSMENT

As you see profits or losses being made, and have up-to-date figures for current assets, then you are in a position to adjust your most recent Balance Sheet to provide a 'draft' picture of your present situation.

What you would *hope* to see would be a greater increase in the assets rather than the liabilities; the balancing item would be an increase in the Profit and Loss Account, and hence your resources base.

Out of the revised picture the lender would look at two major aspects:

- *Gearing*. Hopefully, if you are making profits without having to borrow more to do so, then gearing will improve.
- *Security Cover* — particularly if a Debenture or Floating Charge has been given. The lender will be able to assess the most up-to-date valuation in the light of the type of assets now available, and the type of liabilities against them — bearing in mind that preferential creditors will always rank before the bank. In a Debenture valuation the *quality* of the assets is the prime consideration, so that you should always be ready — whilst not seeking to fool yourself, or hoodwink the lender — to 'sell' the worth of your assets in their best light.

REASONS FOR VARIANCES

These may be many and will not always have been predictable. The lender will understand this and will ask only to be kept informed of material changes, and if appropriate, revised projections.

The message really is do not ignore them, promising yourself that you will assess the position at the end of the year.

A wide difference in the 'actual' column compared with the 'projected' column without reasonable and prompt explanation will make the lender nervous about the accuracy of your future projections.

Again, it's a case of seeing the lender as part of *your* team, and not the opposition. In making sure your lender is fully appraised of variances, you are also disciplining yourself constantly to monitor and understand your progress. You will have your finger firmly on the pulse — vital if you are to succeed.

CONSTANT IMPROVEMENTS

This may seem obvious, but you should always strive to improve upon your performance — increasing your profit margins, turnover and so on.

No matter how well you did last year, the lender will look for at least consistency this year, and will not really be satisfied unless an improving trend is evident.

Again, though, it's important for *you* as much as for keeping the lender happy.

CHANGING MARKETS — DIVERSIFICATION

Successful companies not only keep a tight rein on their own performance; they also keep a close eye on how their competitors are faring and on any changing emphasis in the industry.

Once more, to survive you need to have a broad vision of the overall picture and be ready to diversify into those markets which are most profitable, most in demand, and have a sound outlook.

It's very easy to become blinkered when things are ticking over. But ticking over really means a period of stagnation; opportunities will be missed and profit margins may be running at levels lower than is either possible, or the norm for the industry.

Don't let yourself drift into a position where your market is declining, and your competitors are busily adjusting whilst you stand still.

CHANGING NEEDS

As your market changes, and your diversification programme takes shape, then you must give new attention to your financial needs.

Remember the relevance of matching the type of finance to the specific need, which we discussed earlier, and be ready to have a chat with your lender as matters progress.

To use your agreed overdraft for capital purchases, or to buy another company (whether shares or just assets) is outside of your agreement with the lender. He will expect, quite rightly, to be approached afresh for a new proposal; he will quite naturally be unhappy if you ask for facilities retrospectively.

Each proposal should be supported by a full package along the lines of those discussed earlier.

The lender will probably want an annual review of your various facilities — but don't wait until then before *you* consider the options. It should be constantly at the front of your mind.

THE COST OF FINANCING

As well as remaining alive to the most appropriate finance options open to you, remember that a lender matches the charge for *his* involvement (fee, interest rate etc.) with the risk, security and term.

As your business grows several changes will take place:

- — gearing will improve as profits are retained.
- — liquidity should improve, assuming fixed assets are not purchased from cashflow.
- — security cover will be enhanced by a growing asset base.

In short, as profits are made, your **risk rating** should improve. Likewise, the cost of your borrowing facilities should be reduced — but without your tactful prompting it is unlikely that any such initiative will be taken!

Interest rates, fees and so on are always negotiable. Make sure *you* are in a position to make the running.

CHECKLIST
● Set up monitoring system. ● All aspects covered — liquidity; profitability; balance sheet strength? ● Capitalise on opportunities — full use of creditors; cheaper finance; maximise investments. ● Counter any possible improvements and react. ● Consider, and adapt to market changes. ● Watch competitors; protect your market share. ● Avoid complacency.

11
When Things Go Right

When your business seems to be doing well the last thing you will dream of doing is reading a manual for guidance. This Chapter, therefore, is relatively short; it looks briefly at the points you need to consider to make the most of your success.

NO TIME FOR COMPLACENCY

Never lose sight of the simple fact that your success is due entirely to your own efforts, and to maintain that success you must continue to perform better than your competitors. They will be a constant threat to you and quick to seize any opportunity you give them.

Don't allow your trading record to go to your head. It's only as good as the last contract or sale, and a dissatisfied customer can quickly forget many years of goodwill.

There is no place for complacency. You must keep your finger firmly on the pulse at all times.

CASH MANAGEMENT

As you make profits there will be times — hopefully — when you have a surplus of cash.

Ensure you make full use of it, whether by:

- simple investment, e.g. deposit accounts
- trading growth
- reduced borrowings
- obtaining discounts from early payments to creditors
- capital investment

Consider carefully whether you are likely to need such cash in the foreseeable future for trading, before tying it up permanently in capital items, or repaying loan accounts. If you *are* likely to need it, then keep it liquid, e.g. in a bank deposit account.

Remember — you will normally receive no credit or interest for monies lying in your ordinary bank account. Such balances are an asset and should be made to work.

Make sure you benefit from them.

This is where you need a specialist — usually a qualified accountant — to advise you. Once you are making taxable profits, money spent in employing an accountant is invariably well spent. It needn't cost a fortune, nor will you necessarily be on the telephone to him every hour of the day, but it will pay to find out how to minimise your tax liability.

In fact, a good accountant will often save you more than he charges. For instance, he may advise the use of leasing — often appropriate even before you make profits — or he may suggest the most appropriate Balance Sheet year end for your needs.

He will guide you on the use of writing down allowances, on the purchase of capital item and generally on matters which are straightforward once understood, but a mystery to the uninitiated.

He will help you to make the most from your efforts, and minimise your tax bill.

INVESTING IN THE FUTURE

The successful businessman will have to live for tomorrow, not just for today.

As you grow and make profits now you should be structuring your future plans in terms of:

- projected trading
- projected capital expenditure
- anticipated funding proposals

A five-year plan is often seen as ideal, and whilst this must obviously be treated as flexible it will provide a useful basis for your targets.

It will help you to monitor your short-term progress against your longer term goals, and generally will help you to structure your growth, and plan your investments.

In short, you will know where you are going — or at least *hope* to go!

BUSINESS SALE

It is perhaps a little premature to be considering the sale of the business at this stage, but as matters progress, and the Balance Sheet grows with retained profits, you may wish to divest yourself of part or all of the business and invest in some alternative activity.

Valuation

So how should you value your business, and whom should you approach?

Firstly, valuation will depend upon:

- asset base
- profit performance
- future prospects

A pure asset valuation

This will look simply at the balance sheet value of assets and deduct liabilities. In effect then, you are left with the Resources Base or **Shareholder's Funds**, as the worth of the business. This method, though, ignores the quality of the assets — for example, are the debtors all good? Is the stock all saleable?

It also discounts any **goodwill**. For a going concern with an established patronage (such as a local newsagent or shop) goodwill may be substantial. Conversely a change of ownership may reduce the value of the goodwill markedly. For an asset base valuation, then, you may wish to make adjustments for quality of assets and goodwill.

The performance of the business.

In terms of generated profits in the recent past — say the last five years — this will give an indication of future earnings capacity. If, for example, a 15% net profit margin (before Directors' withdrawals) has traditionally been achieved, then you must consider whether your money could be better invested to obtain a higher return than this.

If you need to borrow to proceed with the purchase, again, will the cost exceed the return — and what will be the effect on your trading viability?

Different industries will expect different levels of profit margin, but as a general rule five times the annual net profit may represent a guide to valuation on a profit performance basis.

Future prospects.

The future prospects of your business may be such that a *premium* can be demanded. A project may have been built up and is now ready to start serious business; it will not necessarily have achieved profitable trading up to now, but the prospects are good. In such a circumstance, where a material change in trading and profit performance is anticipated, then clearly it's appropriate to allow for this in making your valuation.

Finding a Buyer

Secondly, whom should you approach? The introduction and guidance will often come via your solicitor or accountant, but you must decide whether you are most likely to appeal to:

- corporate purchaser
- private investors

A corporate purchaser.
This could be an equity investor interested in buying into your business because they see it as a good 'investment', purely in terms of income. Or it could be a competitor with a complementary function who will see your business as a part of their overall expansion strategy. This may well prove to be the most lucrative sale.

Private investors.
These may take the form of those wishing to benefit from the Business Expansion Scheme in obtaining an equity participation. They may take the form of family investors. They may take the form of contacts introduced by your professional advisers who again either see your business as able to offer a good return in purely monetary terms, or an interest in which they can become actively involved. Where the purchase is seen as a simple investment 'at a distance', then your continued employment, and that of your workers, may be part of the package.

UNLISTED SECURITIES MARKET

We have already discussed the USM as a possible source of finance and divestment of equity (see Chapter 5). Guidance and introductions would be handled by your solicitor, accountant and bank manager, who would usually put you in touch with a merchant banker.

STOCK EXCHANGE QUOTATION

Again, we looked at the opportunities of a full Stock Market listing in Chapter 5. It is unlikely that this will be an appropriate avenue for you in view of the size criteria, but if appropriate you should again channel enquiries through your solicitor, accountant and banker.

CHECKLIST

- Avoid complacency.
- Look for any areas to improve further.
- Ensure market changes don't catch you unawares.
- Maximise opportunities — ensure investments achieve best returns.
- Plan capital expenditure programme for the medium term.
- Plan and monitor future trading aspirations.
- If and when appropriate consider company sale opportunities.

12
When Things Go Wrong

When progress is not as had been hoped and future prospects are threatened, timely remedial action will often be enough to reverse damaging trends.

It is important then to be able to spot the signs of deterioration and react quickly to them.

RECOGNISING THE SIGNS

To be successful you must obviously be making profits, so that any slippage towards losses must be identified quickly.

We have already looked at the relationship between *liquidity* and *profitability* in Chapter 10. In simple terms, and adjusting for any purchases or sales of fixed assets, any profit should bring an improvement in liquidity, whilst any loss should result in a liquidity deterioration.

The first problem, then that you are likely to experience will be:

PRESSURE ON CASHFLOW

Not only will the 'actual' column in the cashflow forecast be showing a noticeable divergence from the 'projection', but you will be wrestling with a more immediate problem — a shortage of cash.

You are likely to be living at the full extent of the Bank overdraft, if you have one, and will be trying to raise cash from anywhere you can, usually by:

- delaying payments to creditors
- seeking early payments from debtors

We have already considered the normal and proper use of this scenario as a source of trading finance, providing there is no adverse reaction from those involved.

The difference between doing this from choice, rather than necessity, is very important.

If from choice, you are in a position to change your approach if there are signs of lost custom, but if you have no choice you will simply have to accept such losses as and when they occur.

In addition to the risks you run of upsetting customers, creditors may prove unwilling to tolerate slower payments. As they begin to press for payment, you will find yourself drifting towards:

- payment schemes
- part payments (usually in round amounts, e.g. £300, which will be very quickly spotted by your Bank Manager who may also be looking for a slice of the cake)
- broken promises aimed at buying time.

Adverse changes in stocking levels may also be a sign that all is not well. An extension in the stock/turnover period may indicate either:

1. Unsaleable stock (possibly out of date)
2. Unwilling purchasers leaving a build-up of stock.

Whilst the main factor therefore is the pure cash shortage, you must also look out for:

3. Extended credit taken with instances of pressing creditors
4. Debtors delaying payments
5. Lost custom/reducing turnover
6. The need to shave profit margins to stay competitive.

THE NEED FOR ACTION

It must be emphasised that it's in your own interest to work *with* your lender — especially when things are not going according to plan.

You will be surprised how tolerant he is. He would certainly prefer to be informed of difficulties whilst the damage is still reversible, rather than later (too late) from a liquidator.

You will fool no-one but yourself if you withhold material facts and try to fob your lender off with broken promises and delaying tactics.

Your lender is a professional and cannot be expected to be taken advantage of; but equally, since he *is* a professional, he will be more than ready to advise you as to the best road to follow.

Your attitude and honesty in the crucial early stages is vital.

Similarly, you must make full use of your accountant, using him as a partner not a competitor; total honesty again plays its part.

THE LENDER'S PERSPECTIVE

Let there be no mistake — the lender *will* wish to see his investment repaid without loss, if necessary by enforcing his security.

He will be in one of two situations:

1. The more usual case is where he has ensured from the outset that he has enough margin of security to cover the worst eventualities. If this is so, *then you may rely on your lender to assist you fully and advise you impartially*.

2. On the other hand, the extent of your difficulties may come somewhat as a surprise to him. Whilst initially he perhaps believed his security would be sufficient, events have proved this not to be the case; as a result of your lower-than-expected performance and depleting asset base he is only partially covered.

   Understandably his attitude will now be highly protective of his own investment, and he will do all he can to improve his position.

   Such moves may involve:

   - pressure to reduce the indebtedness
   - requests for additional security, usually personal such as guarantees.

At the very least he will wish to monitor his position very closely. He will know that your survival may depend upon his willingness to carry an unsatisfactory situation in the hope that things will improve — both in his own, and your, interests. The sort of monitoring he will require is discussed later in this Chapter.

Try to appreciate his perspective and understand the factors which he *must* consider in deciding whether, and how, to support you further.

A DEFINED PLAN

As soon as you know that the trends are deteriorating, do not wait simply for them to improve. The slippage will almost certainly continue beyond the point of no return.

Together with your advisers and lenders — usually your accountant and bank manager — you must work out a **Plan of Action** incorporating:

- all the available options
- sensible and realistic targets
- proposals for monitoring progress.

These points will largely depend upon the specifics of your own situation, but initially the following options should be considered:

1. Is it time to **wind up** the business? If so, delaying whilst further losses are made will only worsen the position.

2. Do you need a **permanent cash injection** to improve gearing and liquidity, while providing additional trading finance without an increase in interest and repayments to damage profit margins? If so, it's time to approach an equity partner as discussed in Chapter 5.
3. Have you taken a hard, close look at your own **profit margins** and **trading patterns**, and compared them to the norm for the industry? It may be that a reduction in your own profit margins could engender sufficient extra turnover to bring about a recovery. But you must look carefully at the break even calculations (see Chapters 2 and 3) before embarking on such a plan and seek the advice of your accountant. The important thing here is to know your market and your competitors.
4. Would a **rearrangement of your finance** help? For instance, if your cashflow is strained but your prospects good, it may be best to try and extend the repayment term of your loan — hence reducing the monthly repayments. A 'solid' element in your overdraft — the amount below which the account never moves — could be refinanced to a loan, to be paid off, say, over a five-year term. This would allow your cashflow, and overdraft, to operate on a more satisfactory basis, and clear the hard core or solid element.
5. A tight cashflow may alternatively be alleviated by factoring.

Once you have weighed up the options open to you, some attention can be given to the new targets you need to achieve.

PERFORMANCE MONITORING

Often your problems will have resulted from a move from profits to losses. You have three aspects to consider:

- What has caused the change?
- What can you do about it?
- What targets are you going to set?

What caused the change?

The slippage will have resulted from one or a combination of:

- a decrease in **trading margins** — perhaps a forced change to stay competitive, but big enough to switch a profitable break-even into a negative one.
- an increase in your **overhead expenses** to such an extent that they can no longer be absorbed by your trading profit.
- a **combination** of the two.

For example, let's take the following starting position:

Gross Trading Profit	£48,000
Overheads	£40,000
Net Profit	£ 8,000

Now, if we consider a 25% slippage in trading profit, then:

Gross Trading Profit	£36,000
Overheads	£40,000
Net Profit (Loss)	(£ 4,000)

or a 25% slippage in overhead expenses:

Gross Trading Profit	£48,000
Overheads	£50,000
Net Profit (Loss)	(£ 2,000)

or a 10% slippage in both trading margins *and* overhead expenses:

Gross Trading Profit	£43,200
Overheads	£44,000
Net Profit (Loss)	(£ 800)

Use of the ratios we looked at in Chapter 10 will help you to identify where the real problems lie. It may be something as simple as Directors' withdrawals growing faster than profits!

It's important to appreciate the distinction between the trading profit, and the overheads charge in monitoring your performance. Be ready to deal with *either*, or *both*, in redressing your profit structure.

What you can do about it.

This will depend largely upon the problem and your own attitude to it.

It may be that the offending slippage *cannot* be rectified. In this case your attention then must be concentrated upon any other areas that can be improved upon. Look for all possible options and give them equal consideration.

Remember the importance of the break-even calculations and that *both* components — the level of sales and the level of profit — will affect the end result.

Remember, too, that the level of sales and prices can go down as well as up, whilst the fixed costs will remain constant.

This gives you the opportunity of reducing prices — remaining competitive — to increase sales and hence profits.

For instance:

Let's assume you can sell 100 items at £10 each (giving £1,000) but fixed costs — rent, rates etc. — are £1,200. You are already expensive, and an increase to £12 for a break-even, or £13 for a profit, will drive customers away. On the other hand, if you cut your price to £7.50 you will be the cheapest supplier, and sales would double. Income would then be £1,500 which, even after fixed costs of £1,200, would still leave you with a profit, despite your price cut.

In reality, of course, life is never so straightforward. You may need new machinery to support the increase in turnover, or additional staff — both of which will erode the profit and cashflow. Even so, an opportunistic approach may be the answer.

It's important that you know how your competitors are thinking, what their profit margins and break-even points are, and how far you yourself can go and still remain viable.

What targets are you going to set?

Whatever you decide it must be supported by an **action plan** setting out defined targets, against which you can monitor progress.

Your targets must be:

- enough to support your viability calculation
- realistic — almost to the point of pessimism.

There is no sense at all in aiming for something which you privately know will be unattainable. Stretch yourself, but do be realistic.

Having set your targets the monitoring process begins. This is just as important as the targets themselves. Only by close and regular assessment will you be able to judge the extent of recovery, and the need for adjustments to your viability plan and targets to make sure it continues.

In the early stages targets and monitoring should be almost daily — certainly weekly — so that you know at all times *exactly* where you stand. Many of the most successful companies in the market today have achieved their position in this way and by knowing when they need to improve competitiveness and indeed can afford to.

LIQUIDITY MONITORING

'I don't understand it — I worked hard, made profits and invested in expansion, yet I faced a cash crisis. It has left me so short of trading finance that I am now on the verge of liquidation!'

It's all very well investing in stock and machinery and offering long credit to customers to make your terms of trade attractive. But if you simply don't have the **cash** to support such an approach, you will soon be juggling the bills to keep your creditors at bay.

If a cash shortage is the problem, then you must look very carefully at the components of your cashflow forecast — looking at each one independently.

For instance, you must ensure that debtors pay on time. If you allow an extra month's credit then you must adjust elsewhere.

It's no comfort at all to your creditors to tell them 'You should be getting the money next month'. They want it now.

It's important, too, in balance sheet terms, that you remain liquid — i.e. have more liquid assets than short term liabilities.

Problems will develop for instance if money collected from debtors is used to buy a fixed asset (machines, cars, etc) before creditors have been settled.

Ideally, your stock, work in progress, and debtors should total more than your Bank debts and creditors — subject to the 'quality of asset' proviso we discussed in Chapter 10. This being the case, in balance sheet terms, your liquidity picture should be acceptable.

The vital point, though, is the availability of cash, and this is what you should concentrate upon.

Security Monitoring

To some extent you may feel that security monitoring is the lender's problem. But an insight into what he is thinking will always give you an added advantage. Security can be split into two categories:

- steady value
- volatile value

Mortgages over fixed assets — houses, land, factories — will generally be regarded as 'steady' and an annual valuation will usually be enough.

Items such as stock and debtors — often the main component of a mortgage debenture — will change value daily. They will depend not only upon the amount outstanding in your books at any one time, but again on the 'quality'. For example:

- the **strength of the debtor** owing you money — can he afford to pay? If not, how much are you likely to receive in a liquidation?
- **The saleability of stock** — is it specialised or out of date? Is there a ready market for it?

For these reasons the lender will want to keep a very close eye on any major movements, and in extending a value will always build in a good margin — as high as 70% in some cases.

It helps if you can work *with* your lender, knowing his perspective, and monitoring the position yourself to know if and when a problem is likely to arise.

This is no time for trying to fool your lender with false valuations — be realistic. An honest approach is far more likely to win additional patience and latitude than is an unhelpful attempt to twist the facts. Lenders are human, too.

Legal Aspects

This is not the place to discuss the intricacies of the Partnership Act or the Companies Act, but you should be aware that there is a fair degree of legislation which affects you, particularly in difficult times — such as **fraudulent preference** and **insolvent trading**.

Your solicitor, or to a lesser degree your bank manager, should be able to offer all the guidance you need.

Working with the Lender

Now, more than any other time, you must see your lender as a partner, and not a competitor.

Usually, the lender will be the main controlling influence and often the deciding factor as to whether you continue in business or not.

With this in mind it is well worth entertaining your lender. There are two things in particular that he will not tolerate:

- dishonesty
- secrecy

Appreciate the commonsense of a full discussion and be ready to listen to and take advice from your bank manager. He has had many years of working with new businesses, and many years of experience in dealing with problems such as your own.

Work with him, not against him.

CHECKLIST

- Recognise the signs— cashflow problems
  — profitability problems
  — liquidity problems.
- Identify the problem
- Consider solution options — terms of trade changes
  — profit margins/break even calculations.
  — alternative types and sources of finance.
- Devise an action plan — set targets and monitor progress.
- Confide in your lender.

13
Who to Contact

LENDING SOURCES

Traditional Banks

A list would be exhaustive. Any High Street Bank will provide you with the addresses of their specialist Small Business experts.

Equity Finance Banks

Again, the list would be exhaustive and any High Street Bank will arrange an introduction.

A major body, owned by all the major Banks is:

Investors in Industry Group,
91 Waterloo Road,
London, SE1 8XP.
Tel: (01) 928 7822

it includes:

City Office
Regional Offices
Venture 3i

but the London office should be able to put you in touch with the right department.

Factoring Companies

The following provide Factoring or Invoice Discounting Services:

Alex. Lawrie Factors Ltd,
(a member of the Lloyds Bank Group),
Beaumont House,
Beaumont Road,
Banbury,
Oxfordshire, OX16 7RN.
Tel: (0295) 67788
(*Branches:* Birmingham, Bristol, Cambridge, Coventry, Edinburgh, Leeds, London, Manchester, Newcastle and Stockport.)

Anglo Factoring Services,
1 Palace Place,
Brighton,
Sussex, BN1 1ET.
Tel: (0273) 21177

Anpal Finance Ltd,
PO Box 37,
Kimberley House,
Vaughan Way,
Leicester, LE1 9AZ.
Tel: (0533) 56066

Arbuthnot Factors Ltd,
Arbuthnot House,
Breeds Place,
Hastings,
Sussex, TN34 3DG.
Tel: (0424) 430824
(*Branches:* Birmingham,
Bristol, Leeds, London,
Manchester, Newcastle and
Nottingham.)

Boston Financial Co. Ltd,
Spencer House,
23 Sheen Road,
Richmond,
Surrey, TW9 1BG.
Tel: (01) 940 4646

Brown Shipley Factors Ltd,
Harlands House,
Haywards Heath,
Sussex, RH16 1TA.
Tel: (0444) 458331

Century Factors Ltd,
60 Princes Street,
Yeovil,
Somerset, BA20 1HL.
Tel: (0935) 76051

Clifton Mercantile Co. Ltd,
115 Gloucester Place,
London, W1H 3PJ.
Tel: (01) 486 0541/2
(Invoice discounting only.)

Credit Factoring International
Ltd,
Smith House,
PO Box 50,
Elmwood Avenue,
Feltham,
Middlesex, TW13 7QD.
Tel: (01) 890 1390
(A member of the National
Westminster Bank Group.
Branches: Birmingham,
Leeds, Manchester.)

Factors Trust Ltd,
UK Business Development,
61 Queen Charlotte Street,
Bristol, BS1 4HQ.
Tel: (0272) 277801

Gaelic Invoice Factors Ltd,
Finlay House,
10-14 West Nile Street,
Glasgow, G1 2PP.
Tel: (041) 248 4901

Griffin Factors Ltd,
(a member of the Midland
Bank Group),
Griffin House,
21 Farncombe Road,
Worthing,
Sussex, BN11 2BW.
Tel: (0903) 205181

H & H Factors Ltd,
Randolph House,
46-48 Wellesley Road,
Croydon,
Surrey, CR9 3PS.
Tel: (01) 681 2641
(*Branches:* Birmingham, Bristol,
Glasgow and Stockport.)

Herebond Ltd,
PO Box 62,
St Mary Abchurch House,
123 Cannon Street,
London, EC4N 5DR.
Tel: (01) 621 1122

International Factors Ltd,
(a member of the Lloyds Bank Group),
Soverign House,
Queen's Road,
Brighton,
Sussex, BN1 3WZ.

Kellock Factors Ltd,
Kellock House,
28 Friar Street,
Reading,
Berkshire, RG1 1DP.
Tel: (0734) 585511

Larosta Ltd,
296 Kingston Road,
London, SW20 8LX.
Tel: (01) 543 3322

London Wall Factors Ltd,
15 South Molton Street,
London, W1Y 1DE.
Tel: (01 408 1502/(0927) 5199

Mansion Factors Ltd,
Mountcliff House,
154 Brent Street,
London, NW4 2DR.

Regent Factors Ltd,
52/56 Osnaburgh Street,
Regent's Park,
London, NW1 3NS.
Tel: (01) 387 4766

Ulster Factors Ltd,
Northern Bank House,
109/113 Royal Avenue,
Belfast, BT1 1FF.
Tel: (0232) 224522

Leasing Companies

A full list of providers can be obtained from the Equipment Leasing Association Ltd, 18 Upper Grosvenor Street, London, W1X 9PB. Telephone: 01 491 2783.

Whichever type of finance you believe to be appropriate, always remember that your bank manager will usually be able to arrange an introduction to an appropriate person.

GOVERNMENT SOURCES

Association of British Chambers of Commerce,
Sovereign House,
212A Shaftesbury Avenue,
London, WC2H 8EW.
Tel: (01) 240 5831

Business in the Community,
227a City Road,
London, EC1V 1LX.
Tel: (01) 253 3716

Council for Small Industries in Rural Areas (CoSIRA),
141 Castle Street,
Salisbury,
Wiltshire, SP1 3TP.
Tel: (0722) 336255
(They will advise local contact point.)

Department of Employment,
Caxton House,
Tothill Street,
London, SW1H 9NF.
Tel: (01) 213 3000

Department of the Environment,
2 Marsham Street,
London, SW1P 3EB.
Tel: (01) 212 3434

Under the direction of the British Overseas Trade Board, The Department of Trade and Industry promotes British exports and exporters, providing an export information service to industry and commerce, and handling government support for overseas trade fairs and promotions. For help or advice contact the nearest regional office of the Department of Trade and Industry:

Department of Trade and Industry,
Room 336,
Kingsgate House,
66-74 Victoria Street,
London, SW1E 6SJ.
Tel: (01) 212 0536/5446/0360

East Midlands
Severns House,
20 Middle Pavement,
Nottingham, NG1 7DW.
Tel: (0602) 506181

North East
Stanegate House,
2 Groat Market,
Newcastle-upon-Tyne,
NE1 1YN.
Tel: (0632) 324722

North West
Sunley Building,
Piccadilly Plaza,
Manchester, M1 4BA.
Tel: (061) 236 2171
or
Merseyside Sub-Office,
Graeme House,
Derby Square,
Liverpool, L2 7UP.
Tel: (051) 227 4111

South East
Ebury Bridge House,
2-18 Ebury Bridge Road,
London, SW1 8QD.
Tel: (01) 730 9678

South West
The Pithay,
Bristol, BS1 2PB.
Tel: (0272) 272666

South West Industrial Development Office,
Phoenix House,
Notte Street,
Plymouth, PL1 2HF.
Tel: (0752) 21891

West Midlands
Ladywood House,
Stephenson Street,
Birmingham, B2 4DT.
Tel: (021) 632 4111

Yorkshire and Humberside
Priestley House,
1 Park Row,
Leeds, LS1 5LF.
Tel: (0532) 443171

Northern Ireland Department of Economic Development,
Netherleigh,
Massey Avenue,
Belfast, BT4 2JP.
Tel: (0232) 63244

Scottish Office,
Alhambra House,
45 Waterloo Street,
Glasgow, G2 6AT.
Tel: (041) 248 2855

Welsh Office,
Industry Department,
New Crown Buildings,
Cathy's Park,
Cardiff, CF1 3NQ.
Tel: (0222) 825111

Welsh Office,
North Wales District Office,
Government Buildings,
Dinerth Road,
Colwyn Bay,
Clwyd, LL28 4UL.
Tel: (0492) 44261

Small Firms Division,
Department of Trade and Industry,
Ashdown House,
123 Victoria Street,
London, SW1E 6RB.
Tel: (01) 212 3395/6

Enterprise Zones
General Information and Regional contacts obtainable from:

Department of the Environment,
Room P2/108,
2 Marsham Street,
London, SW1 3EB.
Tel: (01) 212 7233

Exports Credits Guarantee Department (ECGD)
Headquarters:
Publicity Branch,
Aldermanbury House,
Aldermanbury,
London, EC2P 2EL.
Tel: (01) 382 7777

Crown Building,
Cathays Park,
Cardiff, CF1 3NH.
Tel: (0222) 824100

LEDU — The Small Business Agency for Northern Ireland
LEDU House,
Galwally,
Newtownbreda,
Belfast, BT8 4AR.
Tel: (0232) 691031

Manpower Services Commission (MSC)
Training Division,
Selkirk House,
106 High Holborn,
London, WC1V 6PF.

Training Division,
Companies House,
Crown Way,
Maindy,
Cardiff, CF4 3UT.
Tel: (0222) 388588

Training Division,
9 St Andrew Square,
Edinburgh, EH2 2QX.
Tel: (031) 225 8500

Regional tourist boards
English Tourist Board,
4 Grosvenor Gardens,
London, SW1W 0DU.
Tel: (01) 730 3400

Scottish Tourist Board,
23 Revelston Terrace,
Edinburgh, EH4 3EU.
Tel: (031) 332 2433

Northern Ireland Tourist Board,
River House,
48 High Street,
Belfast, BT1 1DS.
Tel: (0232) 31221

Wales Tourist Board,
Brunel House,
2 Fitzalan Road,
Cardiff, CF2 1UY.
Tel: (0222) 499909

Scottish Development Agency
120 Bothwell Street,
Glasgow, G2 7JP.
Tel: (041) 248 2700

Urban Development Corporations
London Docklands Development Corporation,
Head Office,
Ledger Building,
3 Marsh Wall,
London, E14 9SX.
Tel: (01) 515 3000

Merseyside Development Corporation,
4th Floor,
Royal Liver Building,
Pier Head,
Liverpool,
Merseyside, L3 1JH.
Tel: (051) 236 6090

Welsh Development Agency
Pearl House,
Greyfriars Road,
Cardiff, CF1 3XX.
Tel: (0222) 32955

Regional Development Grant Offices

Queensway House,
West Precinct,
Town Centre,
Billingham,
Cleveland, TS23 2NF.
Tel: (0642) 553671

St Peter's House,
Stanley Precinct,
Bootle,
Merseyside, L20 3LZ.
Tel: (051) 922 4030

24-26 Newport Road,
Cardiff, CF2 1SY.
Tel: (0222) 492611

Magnet House,
59 Waterloo Street,
Glasgow, G2 7BT.
Tel:((041) 221 9833

OTHER BODIES

Insurance Companies

Details can be obtained from:
The Secretary,
Business Finance Information,
c/o British Insurance Association,
Aldermary House,
Queen Street,
London, EC4N 1TU.
Tel: (01) 248 4477

Pension Funds

The Secretary,
The National Association of
Pension Funds Ltd,
12/18 Grosvenor Gardens,
London, SW1H 0DH.
Tel: (01) 730 0585/0734

The Stock Exchange

Details can be obtained from:
The Stock Exchange,
The Quotations Department,
PO Box 119,
London, EC2N 1HE.
Tel: (01) 588 2355
They will also advise local contact points.

Glossary

Arrangement Fee — the charge levied by a lender for interviewing you and setting up a loan or overdraft.

Assisted Areas — areas designated by the Government, which suffer difficult economic conditions, and qualify for various financial support schemes.

Balance Sheet — a summary of the financial affairs of a company at a particular time.

Bankruptcy — the stage when an individual's liabilities exceed his assets and his creditors are unwilling to wait for payment.

Bill of Exchange — a payment document, taking the form of a post-dated cheque, which is widely used in commerce.

Break Even — the stage when the income from a project covers the related expenditure.

Business Expansion Scheme — a scheme run by the Government offering tax concessions on investing in particular types of business.

Capital Repayment Holiday — an arrangement whereby in the first few years of a loan, only the interest is paid with no requirement for any reduction of the actual amount borrowed. Usually the 'holiday' period will be between 2 and 5 years.

Cash Flow — simply the 'flow of your cash' — a chronological list of incomes and expenditures to indicate the amount of cash you will have, or need at any one time.

Charge — the legal provision of some form of security to your lender.

Contract Hire — a specialised form of leasing.

Corporation Tax — a tax on a company's profits — effectively the corporate equivalent of income tax.

Credit — 1. A payment into your account. 2. An arrangement whereby your supplier allows you a period of time before settling his bill, or whereby you allow your customer a similar arrangement.

Creditors — people or companies to which you owe money.

Debenture — a Legal Charge over a company's assets, which will vary in valuation as the level of assets moves up and down.

Debit — a payment out of your account.

Debtors — people or companies who owe you money.

Depreciation — an accounting adjustment to the assets in a balance sheet to reflect their reducing value as time passes.

Dividend — 1. A proportional payment made under a bankruptcy or liquidation representing the final settlement of an outstanding debt. 2. A share of a company's profits received by a shareholder.

Discretion — the limit to which a lender can commit without reference to his superiors.

Enterprise Zones — areas identified by the Government as having growth potential and, as an inducement to attract business there, qualifing for a variety of financial support schemes.

Equity — the element of assets 'owned' by shareholders calculated by deducting the liabilities from the assets. The same as *shareholders funds*.

Equity Options — the option a lender will have, at a future time, to purchase shares in a company to which it has provided facilities, at a pre-set price. Usually part of a venture capital lending package.

Excess — the term used for an element of borrowing above an agreed limit.

Facility — the term used when referring to lending limits.

Factoring — a means of raising money by discounting now monies due over the coming months.

Floating Charge — the same as a mortgage debenture — a charge which 'hovers' over the assets of a company. The value rises and falls as assets move in and out, until the charge is called up at which stage it crystalises.

Freeports — ports where goods may be off-loaded and re-shipped without customs duties and documentation restrictions.

Gearing — the ratio between the amount of assets a company has, and the amount of its borrowing limits.

Going Concern/Gone Concern — the two bases of valuing a company. A 'going concern' basis recognises assets on a full market valuation, whilst a 'gone concern' basis only extends values likely to be achieved in a liquidation auction, usually minimal.

Goodwill — the 'value' in a balance sheet of the good name of the business.

Gross Profit — the trading profit. Simply the cost of sales less the cost of purchases — before heating costs, advertising etc.

Guarantee — a legal agreement whereby an individual agrees to settle someone's, or some company's, liabilities if called upon to do so.

Incoterms — a set of guidance rules published by the International Chamber of Commerce to assist exporters and importers to understand their relative responsibilities.

Indemnity — essentially the same as a guarantee for lending purposes.

Insolvent — the situation when a company's liabilities exceed its assets — i.e. if you sold everything you would still owe money.

Intangible Asset — an asset, such as film rights, or goodwill, which has a worth to the business on a going concern, but which is unlikely to carry a value in the event of a liquidation.

Interest — the cost of borrowing money.

Invoice Discounting — the same sort of arrangement as factoring, but usually bigger figures are involved with fewer debts.

Lease — an arrangement whereby a property (and sometimes an asset) is rented for a specific period. Usually a premium is paid to start with, and sometimes a rental is paid at set times during the term of the *lease*.

Leasing — a method of financing the 'rental' of assets.

Liquidation — the winding up of a Company — all the assets are *liquidated* and creditors paid (as far as possible).

Liquidator — the person nominated to deal with a liquidation.

Liquidity — having more easily-realiseable assets than short-term liabilities (trade creditors, bank overdraft etc). If pressed can you settle all creditors without winding up the company?

Merchant Bank — a bank which concentrates upon large specialist lendings, share dealings and Stock Exchange flotations.

Mortgage — same as a *charge* — but usually refers to property as security.

Net Profit — the bottom line figure — what is left after all deductions. Quoted as either pre-tax, or post tax.

Off Balance Sheet Funding — a means by which assets are obtained for business use, but with neither the funding nor the asset featuring in the balance sheet — for instance rentals, or, in some cases, leasing.

Ordinary Shares — shares in a company. In the event of a liquidation ordinary shareholders are treated as normal creditors when the proceeds of the asset sales are being distributed.

Overdraft — a lending facility appropriate for day to day trading needs to be used when needed on a fluctuating basis.

Overhead — the 'running' costs associated with a particular project or item — i.e. heating, advertising etc.

Postponement of loans — the deferring payment of a specified loan until another loan has been settled.

Preference Shares — the same as ordinary shares except that in the event of liquidation preference shareholders are refunded before ordinary creditors are paid.

Profit — technically a growth of the business; practically, how much money a business can make, but any investment in the business, and reduced value of assets through wear and tear must be considered too.

Profit and Loss Account — the statement summarising the incomes and expenditures of a company over a set period to conclude either with a profit or loss.

Promissory Note — a commercial I.O.U.

Receivership — the personal form of a liquidation — affecting individuals and non-incorporated bodies. The *Receiver* handles the administrative work of the receivership.

Revenue Reserve — the investment in a company which has resulted from retained earned profits.

Risk Capital — money injected into a business as a long term investment representing support for a speculative venture.

Security — the provision to a lender of a Legal Charge over some form of asset (e.g. buildings, stock, debtors etc) enabling him to sell the asset to repay the borrowing if all else fails.

Shareholders Funds — the value of a company's residual assets after deducting all outstanding liabilities. Otherwise known as the 'Surplus Resources'.

Stock Exchange — the market which trades in the purchase and sale of Public Company shares.

Uncleared Effects — a cheque will take usually three days after paying it in to be sure that it has been paid and will not be 'bounced'. During this period the amount of the funds relating to the cheque are referred to as 'uncleared effects', and usually will not be available for drawing against.

Unlisted Securities Market — the baby brother of the Stock Exchange — a market for the sale and purchase of smaller company shares.

Venture Capital — similar to *Risk Capital* — long term financial assistance to support a new (usually) unproven venture, sometimes involving equity options.

Working Capital — monies required for day to day trading — usually provided by overdraft facilities.

Some Useful Reference Books

J. M. Allsopp, *Survival in Business*
Arthur Anderson & Co., *Guide to the Unlisted Securities Market*
Bank of England, *Money for Business*
Bank of England, *Money for Exports*
Bank of England, *Venture Capital in the UK*
D. C. Bloomfield, *Sources of Finance for Small Firms*
E. Davis & J. Pointon, *Finance and the Firm*
Deloitte Haskins & Sells, *Raising Venture Capital*
G. L. R. de Metz, *Off Balance Sheet Finance*
J. Dewhurst & P. Burns, *Small Business — Finance and Control*
A. L. Diamond, *Commercial & Consumer Credit*
H. Edwards, *Export Credit*
W. A. Freyenfeld, *Obtaining Finance for High Technology Ventures*
A. & D. Fowler, *Franchising — A Small Business Guide*
R. L. Hargreaves & R. H. Smith, *Managing your Company's Finances*
M. Monago, *How to Start and Run your own Business*
M. Pitcher, *Management Accounting for the Lending Banker*
M. Richardson, *Going Public*
F. R. Salinger, *Tolley's Factoring*
J. M. Samuels & F. M. Wilkes, *Management of Company Finance*
S. Slatter, *Corporate Recovery*
J. E. Smith, *Cashflow Management*
R. Sowler, *Taxation of Leasing Transactions*
P. Taylor, *How to Keep Business Accounts*
A. Watson, *Finance of International Trade*
C. Woodcock, *Raising Finance — The Guardian Guide for the Small Businessman*

Index

acceptance credit facility, 102
advisory services, 114
architects' certificates, 52
arrangement fee, 32
Assisted Areas, 110

balance sheet assessment, 124
balloon lease, 85
base rate, 8
break even, 28, 37, 38
British Overseas Trade Board (BOTB), 93, 116
British Technology Group, 113
building loans, 51
Business Expansion Scheme, 67, 108
business plan, 23
business sale, 128
business valuation, 129

capital asset purchase, 50
capital base, 12
capital repayment holiday, 10
cashflow forecast, 26, 40, 120
cashflow pressure, 131
cash management, 127
certificates of relief, 108
contract hire, 84, 86
Council for Small Industries in Rural Areas (COSIRA), 111
credit given, 123
creditors, 12
credit risk insurance, 100
credit taken, 124
currency accounts, 94
current ratio, 122

debtors collection, 42
debtors, 12, 31
Department of Employment, 113
Department of Trade, 107
depreciation, 41
Development Areas, 110
development finance, 15, 68
directors' loans, 20
documentary collections, 98
documentary credits, 98

employment linked support, 113
Enterprise Allowance Scheme, 114
Enterprise Zones, 110, 112
equity finance, 66, 70, 72, 139
European Coal and Steel Community, 116
European Investment Bank, 116
European Regional Development Fund, 116
European Social Fund, 117
Export Credit Guarantee Department (ECGD), 100, 103, 116
export factoring, 76, 102
export finance services, 116
export terminology, 95-97

factoring, 15, 76, 139
factory extension loans, 58
Free Ports, 110, 112
fixed term lease, 84
flexible lease, 85
foreign exchange, 93
forfaiting, 103
forward contract, 94
forward option, 94
funds flow (*see also* cashflow), 40

gearing, 20, 66
geographical support, 110
goodwill, 129
government assistance, 73, 107, 141
guarantees, 32

hidden reserves, 20
Highlands and Islands Development Board (HIDB), 111

high technology support, 113
hire purchase, 64, 102

incentives, 108
Incoterms, 95
Inner Urban Areas, 112
insurance companies, 72, 144
intangible assets, 20
interest and fees, 32
interest rates, 10
Intermediate Areas, 110
International Chamber of Commerce, 93
invoice discounting, 76

land, 31
leasing, 16, 64, 83, 141
LEDU, 111
legal aspects, 138
liquidity, 11, 13, 20, 136
liquidity ratio, 123
liquidity trends, 122
loan
  structured, 8
  variable, 8
local authorities aid, 110, 112
Local Enterprise Agencies, 115

management accounts, 120
management buyouts, 67
Management Extension Programme, 114, 115
Manpower Services Commission, 113
margins
  gross profit, 21, 27
net profit, 22, 28
merchant banks, 72
Mid-Wales Development Agency, 111
monthly cashflow forecast, 26, 40, 42

New Enterprise Programme, 115
new towns, 112
NHBC certificates, 52

Office and Service Industries Scheme, 114
office extension loans, 58
open accounts, 97
open-ended lease, 85
overdraft, 7, 35
overhead expenses, 22

pension companies, 72
pricing, 35
profitability, 21
profit forecasts, 26, 38, 121

quasi capital, 12

Regional Selective Assistance, 111
repayment, 28
research and development finance, 65
reserves, 29
running costs, 29
rural and tourism areas, 110

Scottish Development Agency, 111
security, 30, 137
set-off, 9
shareholders' funds, 29, 129
shares, 66
shop purchase loans, 57
Small Firm Loan Guarantee Scheme, 66, 109
Small Firms Service, 114
solvency, 11
source and application of funds, 30
special credits, 99
Special Development Areas, 110
spot rate, 94
standard accounting, 91
start-up capital, 67
stock control, 42
Stock Exchange, 68, 130
stock turnover, 31, 123
structured loans, 8
Support for Innovation Programme, 113

Third Market, 69
timing differences, 26
track record, 19
training schemes, 115
taxation in leasing, 90

Uniform Customs and Practices, 99
Unlisted Securities Market (USM), 69, 130
Urban Development Corporations, 112

valuation of businesses, 129
Value Added Tax, 43
variable rate loans, 8
venture capital, 67
viability, 23, 38

Welsh Development Agency, 111
working capital, 40

Youth Training Schemes, 115